ACTOR'S ULTIMATE

Vol. 1 (Myths and Truths)

Qurate
qurate books.com
Because everyone has a story to tell

Actor's Ultimate- (Myths and Truths) Vol. 1
Kedar Hubli

First Edition

Published in 2024
© Published by

qurate qurateboks.com
Because everyone has a story to tell

Qurate Books Pvt. Ltd.
Goa 403523, India
www.quratebooks.com
Tel: 1800-210-6527, Email: info@quratebooks.com

Page Composition/Typography by GLYPHISBN:

For information, write us at : info@kedarhubli.in
Designed by Kedar Hubli

ISBN: 978-93-58985-37-5

I'd love to thank my mother for her unwavering belief in my dreams provided the foundation for my journey into writing this book about acting. Her constant encouragement and belief in my abilities fueled my passion. Additionally, my mentor's wisdom and guidance have been a wellspring of inspiration, shaping my understanding of the craft and the art of storytelling. Together, their support and inspiration have led me to pen this book on acting.

About the Author

As an enthusiast of the performing arts and a devoted lover of cinema, I find myself influenced by the world of acting. From the tender age of watching black-and-white classics with my family to the technicolor wonders of modern-day blockbusters, my life has been steeped in the magic of the silver screen.

My fascination with acting is not limited to mere entertainment; it's a profound connection that has shaped my identity. I've spent countless hours dissecting performances, analyzing character development, and reveling in the transformative power of the human spirit on display.

But my journey extends beyond the cinema seats. I've immersed myself in acting classes, honing my skills and delving into the psychology of characters. It's a craft that demands empathy, creativity, and an unwavering commitment to the art of storytelling.

Through the years, I've had the privilege of meeting incredible mentors and fellow enthusiasts who have enriched my understanding of acting. Their insights have fueled my passion, and I've found myself not only a spectator but a storyteller in my own right.

Now, as I embark on the journey of writing a book about acting, I am excited to share my experiences, knowledge, and deep-seated admiration for this art form. It's a labor of love, a tribute to the actors who have inspired me, and a testament to the enduring power of storytelling through the lens of a passionate devotee of the silver screen.

-Kedar Hubli

Book Overview

Overview:

In "Myths and Facts about Acting," we delve into the world of acting and debunk common misconceptions surrounding this art form. From the belief that actors are born with natural talent to the notion that acting is all about pretending, this book sets out to separate fact from fiction. By exploring the various techniques, training methods, and skills required for acting, we aim to provide aspiring actors and curious readers with a comprehensive understanding of the craft.

This book challenges the myth that acting is an easy profession. We explore the rigorous training and dedication required to become a successful actor, shedding light on the hard work and perseverance that goes into honing one's craft. Through interviews with experienced actors, we uncover the realities of the industry, offering valuable insights and advice for those considering a career in acting.

"Myths and Facts about Acting" also addresses common misconceptions about the emotional and psychological aspects of acting. We explore the idea that actors must always draw from personal experiences to portray characters authentically, and we provide alternative approaches to emotional connection and character development. By debunking these myths, we hope to inspire actors to explore new techniques and expand their range, ultimately enhancing their performances on stage and screen.

Introduction to Acting

"Acting is behaving truthfully under imaginary circumstances".

- Sanford Meisner

Acting is a form of artistic expression that involves the portrayal of a character or a role through the use of voice, body language, and emotions. It is the art of bringing a written script to life and engaging an audience through the creation of a believable and compelling performance.

Acting is a collaborative art form that involves working closely with directors, fellow actors, and other members of the production team. It requires the ability to listen, adapt, and respond to the cues and dynamics of the ensemble. Acting is not a solitary endeavor; it is a collective effort to create a cohesive and impactful performance.

While acting often involves memorizing lines and following a script, it is not simply a matter of reciting words. Actors must bring depth, nuance, and authenticity to their performances. They must understand the motivations, desires, and conflicts of their characters and find ways to convey them convincingly.

TABLE OF CONTENTS

TABLE OF CONTENTS

Page left blank intentionally

PART ONE

WHAT IS ACTING??

Acting is a continuous process of exploration and discovery. It requires ongoing training, practice, and self-reflection to refine and expand one's skills. Actors must be open to feedback and willing to push their boundaries in order to grow as performers.

One of the key aspects of acting is the ability to live truthfully under imaginary circumstances. Actors must be able to suspend their own beliefs and immerse themselves in the world of the character. This requires a high level of imagination, creativity, and the willingness to take risks.

In summary, acting is the art of embodying a character and bringing their story to life through the use of voice, body language, and emotions. It is a form of storytelling that requires technical skill, artistic sensibility, and a deep understanding of human behavior. Acting is a collaborative endeavor that involves working closely with others to create compelling and authentic performances. It is a continuous journey of exploration and growth, requiring ongoing training and self-reflection.

CHAPTER 1

THE IMPORTANCE OF ACTING

Acting is a powerful and essential art form that has been a part of human culture for centuries. It plays a crucial role in various aspects of society, including entertainment, education, therapy, and communication. In this section, we will explore the importance of acting and how it impacts individuals and society as a whole.

Expressing Emotions and Telling Stories

One of the primary functions of acting is to express emotions and tell stories. Through the portrayal of characters and their experiences, actors have the ability to evoke a wide range of emotions in their audience. Whether it's joy, sadness, anger, or fear, acting allows individuals to connect with their own emotions and empathize with the experiences of others. This emotional connection is what makes acting such a powerful and transformative art form.

Acting also serves as a means of storytelling. It allows actors to bring characters to life and communicate narratives in a compelling and engaging way. Whether it's on stage, in film, or on television, acting enables the audience to experience different worlds, cultures, and perspectives. It has the power to challenge societal norms, provoke thought, and inspire change.

Building Empathy and Understanding

Acting has the unique ability to foster empathy and understanding among individuals. By stepping into the shoes of a character, actors gain a deeper understanding of human emotions, motivations, and experiences. This understanding translates into their performances, allowing the audience to connect with the characters on a profound level.

Through acting, individuals can explore different perspectives and challenge their own biases and preconceptions. It encourages open-mindedness and promotes a more inclusive and compassionate society. By witnessing the struggles and triumphs of characters, audiences can develop a greater appreciation for the diversity of human experiences.

Developing Communication and Social Skills

Acting is not only about performing on stage or in front of a camera; it also plays a significant role in developing communication and social skills. Actors must learn to effectively communicate with their fellow cast members, directors, and crew members. They must listen, respond, and collaborate to create a cohesive and compelling performance.

Acting also requires individuals to be aware of their body language, voice, and facial expressions. Through training and practice, actors learn to use these tools to convey meaning and emotion. These skills are not only valuable on stage but also in everyday life. The ability to communicate effectively, express oneself clearly, and understand non-verbal cues are essential in personal and professional relationships.

Boosting Confidence and Self-Esteem

Engaging in acting can have a profound impact on an individual's confidence and self-esteem. Through the process of embodying different characters and performing in front of an audience, actors learn to overcome stage fright and develop a sense of self-assurance. They gain the ability to project their voice, command attention, and captivate an audience.

Acting also provides a platform for individuals to explore and express their own unique identities. It allows them to embrace their strengths, confront their weaknesses, and celebrate their individuality. This self-exploration and self-expression can lead to increased self-awareness and a greater sense of self-worth.

Promoting Cultural Exchange and Diversity

Acting has the power to promote cultural exchange and celebrate diversity. It allows individuals from different backgrounds to share their stories, traditions, and perspectives with a global audience. Through the portrayal of diverse characters, actors challenge stereotypes and promote understanding and acceptance of different cultures.

By showcasing a wide range of experiences and identities, acting encourages inclusivity and representation. It provides a platform for underrepresented voices to be heard and celebrated. This diversity in storytelling not only enriches the art form but also contributes to a more inclusive and equitable society.

In conclusion, acting is not just about entertainment; it is a vital and transformative art form that impacts individuals and society in numerous ways. It allows for the expression of emotions, the telling of stories, the development of empathy and understanding, the enhancement of communication and social skills, the boosting of confidence and self-esteem, and the promotion of cultural exchange and diversity. Acting has the power to inspire, educate, and provoke change, making it an essential and valuable part of our world.

CHAPTER 2

THE HISTORY OF ACTING

Acting is an art form that has been around for centuries, with its roots dating back to ancient civilizations. The history of acting is a fascinating journey that showcases the evolution of this craft and its significance in various cultures and societies.

Ancient Origins

The origins of acting can be traced back to ancient civilizations such as ancient Greece and Rome. In these societies, acting was an integral part of religious rituals and festivals. Performers would portray gods, goddesses, and mythical characters to entertain and educate the audience.

Greek theater, in particular, played a significant role in the development of acting. The ancient Greeks believed in the power of theater to explore human emotions and moral dilemmas. The renowned playwrights of the time, such as Sophocles and Euripides, wrote plays that delved into complex themes and showcased the talents of actors.

Medieval Theater

During the Middle Ages, acting took on a different form. The church played a dominant role in society, and religious dramas known as mystery plays and miracle plays became popular. These plays depicted biblical stories and were performed by clergy and members of religious guilds.

Acting during this period was highly stylized and focused on conveying moral messages to the audience. The performers used exaggerated gestures and vocal techniques to engage the spectators and bring the stories to life.

Renaissance and Elizabethan Theater

The Renaissance period marked a significant shift in acting styles. The emergence of humanism and the revival of classical Greek and Roman texts led to a renewed interest in theater. Playwrights like William Shakespeare revolutionized the art of acting with their complex characters and intricate plots.

Actors during the Elizabethan era faced unique challenges. The theaters were open-air, and the actors had to project their voices and gestures to reach the entire audience. The famous Globe Theatre in London became a hub for theatrical performances, and actors like Richard Burbage and Edward Alleyn gained fame for their exceptional skills.

The Birth of Realism

In the 19th century, a new movement called realism emerged in theater. Playwrights and actors sought to portray life as it truly was, focusing on naturalistic performances and believable characters. This marked a departure from the exaggerated styles of the past.

One of the key figures in the development of realism was Konstantin Stanislavski, a Russian actor and director. Stanislavski believed in the importance of psychological realism and developed a system of acting techniques that emphasized emotional truth and authenticity.

The Rise of Method Acting

In the 20th century, method acting gained prominence, thanks to the work of influential actors such as Lee Strasberg and Stella Adler.

Method acting is a technique that encourages actors to draw from their own personal experiences and emotions to create realistic performances.

Method actors immerse themselves in the lives of their characters, often conducting extensive research and adopting specific physical and vocal traits. This approach revolutionized the acting industry and gave birth to some of the most memorable performances in film and theater history.

Contemporary Acting

Today, acting continues to evolve and adapt to the changing times. With advancements in technology and the rise of digital media, actors now have opportunities to showcase their talents in various mediums, including film, television, and online platforms.

Acting schools and training programs have also become more accessible, allowing aspiring actors to learn and develop their skills. The industry has become more diverse and inclusive, with actors from different backgrounds and cultures making their mark on the global stage.

In conclusion, the history of acting is a rich tapestry that spans centuries and cultures. From ancient rituals to modern-day performances, acting has always been a powerful means of storytelling and self-expression. As the art form continues to evolve, actors will undoubtedly shape the future of this captivating craft.

CHAPTER 3

THE ROLE OF THE ACTOR

Acting is a complex and multifaceted art form that requires a deep understanding of human emotions, physicality, and the ability to bring characters to life. In this section, we will explore the role of the actor and the various responsibilities they have in the world of acting.

The Interpreter of Stories

At its core, the role of the actor is to be the interpreter of stories They are the ones who bring the words on a page to life, giving them depth, emotion, and meaning. Whether it's on in film, or on television actors have the power to transport audiences into different worlds and make them believe in the characters they portray.

Bringing Characters to Life

One of the primary responsibilities of an actor is to bring characters to life. They must fully embody the thoughts, emotions, and physicality of the character they are portraying. This requires a deep understanding of the character's background, motivations, and desires. Actors must be able to tap into their own emotions and experiences to create a believable and authentic portrayal.

Emotional Truth

Actors are often tasked with portraying a wide range of emotions, from joy and love to anger and sadness. It is their responsibility to convey these emotions in a way that is truthful and relatable to the audience. This requires a deep understanding of human emotions and the ability to tap into their own emotional well-being. By connecting with their own emotions, actors can create performances that resonate with audiences on a profound level.

Collaboration

Acting is not a solitary art form. Actors must work closely with directors, fellow actors, and the production team to bring a performance to life. Collaboration is essential in creating a cohesive and compelling production. Actors must be able to take direction, adapt to different styles, and work well with others to create a harmonious and successful production.

Continuous Learning and Growth

The role of the actor is not static. It is a lifelong journey of continuous learning and growth. Actors must constantly seek out opportunities to expand their skills, whether through acting classes, workshops, or by working with different directors and co-actors. They must be open to feedback and criticism, always striving to improve their craft and push the boundaries of their abilities.

Versatility

Actors are often required to play a wide range of characters, from heroes to villains, from young to old, and from different time periods and cultures. This requires a high level of versatility and the ability to adapt to different roles and styles of acting. Actors must be able to transform themselves physically, vocally, and emotionally to convincingly portray a diverse range of characters.

Captivating an Audience

Ultimately, the role of the actor is to captivate an audience. Whether it's through a powerful monologue, a heartfelt scene, or a comedic performance, actors have the ability to evoke strong emotions and create a connection with the audience. They have the power to transport people to different worlds, and make them laugh, cry, and think. The ability to captivate an audience is a testament to the skill and dedication of the actor.

Advocacy and Representation

Actors also have the opportunity to use their platform to advocate for social issues and promote representation and diversity in the entertainment industry. By portraying characters from different backgrounds and experiences, actors can help break down stereotypes and challenge societal norms. They have the power to inspire change and create a more inclusive and equitable industry.

PART TWO

THE BASICS OF ACTING

CHAPTER 3

THE ROLE OF THE ACTOR

Understanding Emotions

Acting is a craft that requires the ability to tap into and express a wide range of emotions. Understanding emotions is a fundamental aspect of acting, as it allows actors to connect with their characters and portray them authentically. In this section, we will explore the importance of understanding emotions in acting and discuss techniques that actors can use to effectively convey emotions on stage or screen.

The Importance of Emotions in Acting

Emotions are the driving force behind human behavior, and they play a crucial role in storytelling. As an actor, your job is to bring characters to life and make their experiences relatable to the audience. To achieve this, you must have a deep understanding of emotions and how they manifest in different situations.

Emotions are complex and multi-faceted, ranging from joy and love to anger and sadness. Each emotion carries its own unique energy and physicality, and it is the actor's responsibility to accurately convey these emotions through their performance. By understanding emotions, actors can create believable characters that resonate with the audience on an emotional level.

Emotional Awareness and Observation

To effectively portray emotions, actors must first develop emotional awareness. This involves being in tune with their own emotions and being able to recognize and understand the emotions of others. Emotional awareness allows actors to draw from their own experiences and observations to create authentic performances.

Observation is a key skill for actors when it comes to understanding emotions. By observing people in real-life situations, actors can study how emotions are expressed through body language, facial expressions, and vocal tone. Paying attention to the nuances of emotions in everyday life can provide valuable insights that can be applied to acting.

Emotional Memory and Recall

One technique that actors use to access emotions is emotional memory or recall. Emotional memory involves tapping into personal experiences and memories to evoke specific emotions. By drawing on their own emotional reservoir, actors can bring a sense of truth and authenticity to their performances.

To effectively use emotional memory, actors must be able to recall past experiences and emotions in a controlled and safe manner. This requires a strong sense of self-awareness and emotional stability. Actors often work with acting coaches or therapists to develop techniques for accessing and channeling emotions in a healthy and controlled way.

Emotional Substitution

Another technique that actors use to understand and portray emotions is emotional substitution. This involves substituting personal emotions with the emotions of the character they are portraying. By finding similarities between their own experiences and the character's circumstances, actors can tap into genuine emotions that resonate with the audience.

Emotional substitution requires empathy and the ability to put oneself in someone else's shoes. It allows actors to connect with the character's emotional journey and bring a depth of understanding to their performance. However, it is important for actors to maintain a clear distinction between their own emotions and those of the character to avoid becoming overwhelmed or losing their sense of self.

Physicality and Emotion

Emotions are not just felt internally; they also manifest physically. The body and emotions are interconnected, and actors must be able to express emotions through their physicality. Physicality includes body language, gestures, posture, and movement.

By understanding the physical manifestations of different emotions, actors can enhance their performances and make them more believable. For example, a character experiencing anger may have tense muscles, clenched fists, and a rigid posture. On the other hand, a character experiencing joy may have an open and relaxed body, with fluid movements and a smile.

Vocal Expression of Emotion

In addition to physicality, vocal expression is a powerful tool for conveying emotions in acting. The tone, pitch, volume, and rhythm of the voice can all be used to communicate different emotional states. Actors must be able to modulate their voices to accurately reflect the emotions of their characters.

For example, a character experiencing fear may have a higher-pitched voice, speak quickly, and have a trembling quality to their voice. Conversely, a character experiencing sadness may have a lower-pitched voice, speak slowly, and have a softer tone. By understanding the vocal nuances of emotions, actors can bring depth and authenticity to their performances.

Emotional Flexibility and Range

As an actor, it is important to develop emotional flexibility and range. This means being able to access and portray a wide spectrum of emotions, from the subtle to the intense. Emotional flexibility allows actors to adapt to different characters and situations, and it adds depth and complexity to their performances.

To develop emotional flexibility, actors can engage in exercises and improvisations that challenge them to explore different emotional states. This can involve working with scene partners, participating in acting classes, or engaging in solo exercises that focus on emotional exploration. By continuously expanding their emotional range, actors can become more versatile and compelling performers.

Conclusion

Understanding emotions is a fundamental aspect of acting. By developing emotional awareness, utilizing techniques such as emotional memory and substitution, and exploring the physical and vocal expressions of emotions, actors can create authentic and compelling performances. Emotional flexibility and range are essential for portraying a wide variety of characters and connecting with audiences on a deep emotional level. As an actor, investing time and effort into understanding emotions will greatly enhance your craft and allow you to bring characters to life in a powerful and meaningful way.

CHAPTER 4
PHYSICALITY AND MOVEMENT

Physicality and movement are essential elements of acting that help bring a character to life on stage or screen. While emotions and dialogue play a significant role in conveying a character's thoughts and feelings, the way an actor moves and carries themselves can communicate just as much, if not more, to the audience. In this section, we will explore the importance of physicality and movement in acting and discuss various techniques that actors use to enhance their performances.

The Importance of Physicality

Physicality refers to the way an actor uses their body to express emotions, convey character traits, and communicate with the audience. It involves the actor's posture, gestures, facial expressions, and overall movement. By paying attention to their physicality, actors can create a more believable and engaging performance.

One of the primary reasons physicality is crucial in acting is that it helps the audience understand the character's intentions and emotions. For example, a character who is confident and powerful may stand tall with a straight posture, while a character who is timid or fearful may hunch their shoulders and avoid eye contact. These physical choices provide visual cues to the audience, allowing them to connect with the character on a deeper level.

Physicality also helps actors differentiate between characters. Each character has a unique physical presence that sets them apart from others. By consciously adjusting their physicality, actors can transform themselves into different characters, making each one distinct and memorable.

Techniques for Enhancing Physicality

There are several techniques that actors use to enhance their physicality and movement skills. These techniques help actors develop a greater awareness of their bodies and enable them to make deliberate choices that serve the character and the story.

Body Awareness: Developing body awareness is the foundation of physicality in acting. Actors must understand how their bodies move and how different movements can convey different emotions or character traits. This can be achieved through exercises such as yoga, dance, or physical warm-ups that focus on stretching and loosening the body.

Observation: Observing and studying human behavior is another valuable technique for enhancing physicality. By observing how people move, gesture, and carry themselves in different situations, actors can incorporate these nuances into their performances. This includes studying body language, facial expressions, and even the way people walk.

Laban Movement Analysis: Laban Movement Analysis is a technique developed by Rudolf Laban that focuses on understanding and analyzing different qualities of movement. It categorizes movement into four main components: body, effort, shape, and space. By exploring these components, actors can create a more nuanced and expressive physicality for their characters.

Viewpoints: Viewpoints is a technique developed by Anne Bogart and the SITI Company that emphasizes the relationship between time and space in performance. It encourages actors to explore different physical choices by considering elements such as tempo, shape, gesture, and spatial relationships. Viewpoints can help actors develop a heightened sense of physical presence and awareness.

Alexander Technique: The Alexander Technique is a method that focuses on improving posture, balance, and coordination. It helps actors release tension and develop a more relaxed and aligned physicality. By practicing the Alexander Technique, actors can improve their overall physical presence and prevent physical habits that may hinder their performances.

When developing a character, actors must consider how physicality can contribute to the portrayal. Physicality can reveal a character's age, occupation, social status, and even their emotional state. By making conscious choices about how a character moves and carries themselves, actors can deepen their understanding of the character and create a more authentic performance.

To incorporate physicality into character development, actors can start by asking themselves a series of questions:

- How does the character stand or sit?
- What are their typical gestures or mannerisms?
- How do they use their body to express emotions?
- Are there any physical limitations or disabilities that affect their movement?
- How does the character's physicality change throughout the story?
- By exploring these questions and experimenting with different physical choices, actors can develop a physicality that aligns with the character's personality, background, and circumstances.

In conclusion, physicality and movement are vital aspects of acting that help actors bring their characters to life. By paying attention to their body language, gestures, and overall movement, actors can effectively communicate a character's thoughts, emotions, and intentions to the audience. Through various techniques and exercises, actors can enhance their physicality skills and create more compelling and believable performances. Incorporating physicality into character development allows actors to deepen their understanding of the character and create a more authentic portrayal.

CHAPTER 5
VOICE AND DICTION

Voice and diction are essential elements of acting that can greatly enhance a performer's ability to effectively communicate with an audience. While physicality and facial expressions play a significant role in conveying emotions, the voice is the primary tool for delivering dialogue and expressing the inner thoughts and feelings of a character. In this section, we will explore the importance of voice and diction in acting and discuss techniques to improve vocal performance.

The Importance of Voice and Diction

A strong and well-trained voice is crucial for an actor to effectively portray a character and engage the audience. The voice carries the emotional depth and nuances of a performance, allowing the audience to connect with the character on a deeper level. It is through the voice that an actor can convey the thoughts, desires, and conflicts of a character, bringing them to life.

Diction, on the other hand, refers to the clarity and articulation of speech. It is essential for actors to have clear diction to ensure that their words are understood by the audience. Poor diction can hinder the audience's comprehension of the story and the character's intentions, leading to a breakdown in communication.

Techniques to Improve Voice and Diction

Breathing and Vocal Warm-ups: Proper breathing techniques are fundamental for developing a strong and resonant voice. Actors often engage in breathing exercises to expand their lung capacity and improve breath control. Vocal warm-ups, such as humming, lip trills, and tongue twisters, can help to relax the vocal cords and prepare them for performance.

Articulation Exercises: Clear articulation is crucial for effective communication. Actors can practice exercises that focus on enunciating each syllable and consonant, such as tongue twisters and vowel exercises. These exercises help to improve clarity and precision in speech.

Projection and Resonance: Projection refers to the ability to make the voice carry to the back of the audience without straining. Resonance, on the other hand, involves using the natural resonance chambers of the body to create a rich and full sound. Techniques such as vocal placement and resonance exercises can help actors develop a powerful and resonant voice.

Vocal Variety: A skilled actor can use their voice to convey a wide range of emotions and create distinct characters. By varying pitch, tone, and pace, actors can bring depth and complexity to their performances. Practicing vocal exercises that focus on exploring different vocal qualities and emotions can help actors develop versatility in their voices.

Dialect and Accent Training: Depending on the character and the setting of a production, actors may need to adopt specific dialects or accents. Dialect and accent training involves studying the speech patterns, intonation, and pronunciation of a particular region or culture. Working with a dialect coach or using online resources can help actors develop authentic and convincing accents.

Applying Voice and Diction in Acting

Once actors have developed a strong foundation in voice and diction, they can apply these skills to their performances. Here are some ways in which voice and diction can enhance an actor's portrayal of a character:

Characterization: The voice can be used to reflect the personality, background, and emotional state of a character. By adjusting vocal qualities such as pitch, tone, and rhythm, actors can create distinct voices for each character they portray.

Emotional Expression: The voice is a powerful tool for expressing emotions. By modulating vocal qualities, actors can convey a wide range of emotions, from joy and excitement to sadness and anger. The voice can add depth and authenticity to the emotional journey of a character.

Storytelling: Clear diction and effective vocal delivery are crucial for storytelling. Actors must ensure that their words are understood by the audience, allowing them to follow the narrative and connect with the characters and their experiences.

Stage Presence: A strong and confident voice can enhance an actor's stage presence. It helps to command attention and engage the audience, creating a captivating performance.

In conclusion, voice and diction are vital components of acting that contribute to the overall effectiveness of a performance. By developing a strong and well-trained voice, actors can effectively communicate with the audience, convey the thoughts and emotions of their characters, and bring their performances to life. Through proper breathing, articulation, projection, and vocal variety, actors can enhance their vocal performance and create memorable and impactful characters on stage or screen.

CHAPTER 6
CHARACTER DEVELOPMENT

Character development is a crucial aspect of acting that involves creating and portraying believable and compelling characters on stage or screen. It is the process through which actors bring their characters to life, giving them depth, complexity, and authenticity. By understanding their characters' motivations, emotions, and relationships, actors can effectively communicate their stories to the audience.

Understanding the Character

Before diving into the process of character development, actors must first thoroughly understand the character they are portraying. This involves studying the script and analyzing the character's background, personality traits, desires, and conflicts. By delving into the character's history, relationships, and experiences, actors can gain insights into their motivations and behaviors.

To understand the character better, actors can ask themselves a series of questions:

- What is the character's backstory?
- What are their goals and desires?
- What are their strengths and weaknesses?
- What are their relationships with other characters?
- What are their fears and insecurities?
- What are their physical and emotional traits?
- By answering these questions, actors can develop a deeper understanding of their characters, allowing them to portray them more convincingly.

Building the Physicality

Physicality plays a significant role in character development. How a character moves, stands, and gestures can reveal a lot about their personality, emotions, and background. Actors must pay attention to their body language and explore how their characters would physically express themselves.

To develop the physicality of a character, actors can consider the following:

Posture: How does the character hold themselves? Are they confident, slouched, or rigid?
Gestures: What kind of gestures does the character use? Are they expressive, reserved, or specific to their background?
Movement: How does the character move? Are they graceful, clumsy, or have a unique way of walking?
Facial Expressions: What emotions does the character display on their face? Are they expressive or more guarded?
By experimenting with different physical choices, actors can find the right balance that aligns with their character's personality and story.

Emotional Connection

Emotional connection is at the heart of character development. Actors must tap into their own emotions and find ways to connect with their characters' feelings and experiences. By understanding the emotional journey of their characters, actors can bring authenticity and depth to their performances.

To establish an emotional connection with their characters, actors can:

- **Relate to personal experiences**: Find similarities between their own experiences and those of their characters.
- **Use imagination**: Imagine themselves in the character's situation and explore how they would feel.
- **Empathy**: Develop empathy towards the character's circumstances and emotions.
- By accessing their own emotions and understanding the emotional landscape of their characters, actors can create performances that resonate with the audience.

Relationships and Interactions

Characters do not exist in isolation; they interact with other characters within the story. Understanding the relationships and dynamics between characters is essential for character development. Actors must explore the connections, conflicts, and emotions that arise from these relationships.

To develop the relationships and interactions of their characters, actors can:

- **Study the script**: Analyze the dialogue and subtext to understand the nuances of the relationships.
- **Rehearse with co-actors**: Collaborate with fellow actors to develop chemistry and explore the dynamics between characters.
- **Explore power dynamics**: Understand the power imbalances and conflicts that may exist between characters.

By delving into the relationships and interactions of their characters, actors can create more authentic and compelling performances.

Continual Exploration and Growth

Character development is an ongoing process that requires continual exploration and growth. As actors gain more experience and knowledge, they can refine their techniques and deepen their understanding of their characters. It is essential to remain open to new ideas, feedback, and opportunities for growth.

Actors can continue to develop their characters by:

- **Seeking feedback**: Collaborate with directors, acting coaches, and fellow actors to gain insights and perspectives on their performances.
- **Experimenting**: Try different approaches, techniques, and interpretations to discover new layers to their characters.
- **Reflecting**: Take time to reflect on their performances and identify areas for improvement.

By embracing a growth mindset and continually honing their craft, actors can enhance their character development skills and deliver more nuanced and captivating performances.

Character development is a fundamental aspect of acting that allows actors to create memorable and impactful performances. By understanding their characters' motivations, physicality, emotions, and relationships, and continually exploring their growth, actors can bring depth and authenticity to their roles. Through the process of character development, actors can connect with their characters on a profound level and effectively communicate their stories to the audience.

PART THREE

METHODS OF ACTING

CHAPTER 7

THE STANISLAVSKI SYSTEM

The Stanislavski System, also known as the Method, is one of the most influential and widely practiced methods of acting. Developed by the Russian actor and director Konstantin Stanislavski in the late 19th and early 20th centuries, this approach revolutionized the way actors approached their craft. The Stanislavski System emphasizes the importance of psychological realism, emotional truth, and the actor's ability to fully immerse themselves in the character and the given circumstances of the play.

The Origins of the Stanislavski System

Konstantin Stanislavski was a visionary who sought to create a more authentic and believable form of acting. He believed that actors should not simply imitate or pretend, but rather tap into their own emotions and experiences to create truthful and compelling performances. Stanislavski's ideas were shaped by his own experiences as an actor and his observations of the shortcomings of the acting techniques of his time.

The Pillars of the Stanislavski System

The Stanislavski System is built upon several key principles that guide actors in their approach to creating a character and delivering a performance. These principles include:

Emotional Memory: Stanislavski believed that actors should draw upon their own personal experiences and emotions to connect with the emotions of their characters. By tapping into their own memories and feelings, actors can create a genuine emotional response that resonates with the audience.

Given Circumstances: Understanding the given circumstances of the play, including the time, place, and social context, is crucial for actors to fully immerse themselves in the world of the character. By thoroughly analyzing the script and the character's background, actors can make informed choices that align with the character's circumstances.

Objective and Super-Objective: Stanislavski emphasized the importance of defining the character's objectives and super-objective. The objective is the character's immediate goal in a particular scene, while the super-objective is the character's overarching goal throughout the entire play. By understanding these objectives, actors can bring clarity and purpose to their performances.

Action and Tactics: Stanislavski believed that actors should focus on the character's actions and tactics rather than simply portraying emotions. By identifying the character's actions and the tactics they employ to achieve their objectives, actors can create dynamic and engaging performances.

Sense of Truth and Believability: The Stanislavski System places a strong emphasis on creating a sense of truth and believability on stage. Actors are encouraged to fully commit to their characters and the given circumstances, allowing the audience to suspend their disbelief and become fully engaged in the story.

Techniques and Exercises

The Stanislavski System offers a range of techniques and exercises to help actors develop their skills and fully embody their characters. Some of these techniques include:

Emotional Memory: Actors are encouraged to recall personal memories and emotions that align with the emotions of their characters. By reliving these memories, actors can tap into genuine emotions and bring authenticity to their performances.

Magic If: This technique involves asking "What if?" questions to explore the character's motivations and actions. By imagining different scenarios and possibilities, actors can deepen their understanding of the character and make more informed choices.

Given Circumstances Analysis: Actors thoroughly analyze the given circumstances of the play, including the time, place, and social context. This analysis helps actors make informed choices about their characters' behaviors, motivations, and relationships.

Physical Actions: Actors focus on the physical actions their characters perform on stage. By connecting the character's actions to their objectives, actors can create a more dynamic and engaging performance.

Inner Monologue: This technique involves developing an inner dialogue for the character, allowing actors to explore the character's thoughts, desires, and motivations. By understanding the character's inner world, actors can bring depth and complexity to their performances.

Impact and Legacy

The Stanislavski System has had a profound impact on the world of acting and continues to be widely practiced and studied today. It has influenced countless actors, directors, and acting techniques, including the Meisner Technique, the Method Acting Approach, and the Brechtian Approach.

By emphasizing psychological realism, emotional truth, and a deep understanding of the character and the given circumstances, the Stanislavski System has helped actors create more nuanced and authentic performances. It has also contributed to the development of a more collaborative and ensemble-based approach to theater, where actors work closely with directors and fellow actors to create a cohesive and compelling production.

In conclusion, the Stanislavski System is a comprehensive and influential approach to acting that has shaped the way actors approach their craft. By focusing on psychological realism, emotional truth, and a deep understanding of the character and the given circumstances, actors can create more authentic and compelling performances. The techniques and principles of the Stanislavski System continue to be invaluable tools for actors seeking to fully immerse themselves in their characters and deliver powerful and memorable performances.

CHAPTER 8
THE MEISNER TECHNIQUE

The Meisner Technique is a widely recognized and influential approach to acting that was developed by Sanford Meisner, an American actor and acting teacher. This technique focuses on the actor's ability to fully immerse themselves in the present moment and respond truthfully to their fellow actors and the given circumstances of the scene. It is a method that emphasizes spontaneity, emotional truth, and the exploration of human behavior.

The Origins of the Meisner Technique

Sanford Meisner began his career as an actor in the Group Theatre, a groundbreaking theater company in New York City during the 1930s. He worked alongside influential figures such as Lee Strasberg and Stella Adler, who were also developing their own acting techniques. Meisner's approach to acting was heavily influenced by the teachings of Russian theater director Konstantin Stanislavski, particularly his emphasis on emotional truth and the actor's connection to their fellow performers.

The Foundation of the Meisner Technique

At the core of the Meisner Technique is the concept of "the repetition exercise." This exercise involves two actors facing each other and repeating simple phrases or actions while observing and responding to each other's behavior. The purpose of this exercise is to develop the actor's ability to listen and respond truthfully in the moment, without preconceived ideas or predetermined emotions. Through the repetition exercise, actors learn to focus on their partner's behavior and allow their own emotional responses to arise naturally. This helps them to develop a heightened sense of awareness and authenticity in their performances. The repetition exercise also serves as a foundation for the exploration of more complex scenes and characters.

Emotional Preparation and Imaginary Circumstances

In addition to the repetition exercise, the Meisner Technique places a strong emphasis on emotional preparation and the use of imaginary circumstances. Actors are encouraged to delve deep into their own emotional experiences and memories to create a rich inner life for their characters. By connecting with their own emotions, actors can bring a sense of truth and depth to their performances.

Imaginary circumstances are also an essential component of the Meisner Technique. Actors are encouraged to vividly imagine the given circumstances of the scene, including the time, place, and relationships between characters. This helps them to fully immerse themselves in the world of the play and create authentic and believable performances.

Active Listening and Moment-to-Moment Acting

One of the key principles of the Meisner Technique is active listening. Actors are taught to listen intently to their scene partners, not only to their words but also to their emotional cues and subtext. This allows them to respond truthfully and spontaneously in the moment, rather than relying on pre-planned reactions or line readings.

By practicing active listening, actors develop a heightened sense of presence and responsiveness. They learn to trust their instincts and allow their emotions to guide their performances. This creates a dynamic and organic quality in their acting, as they are fully engaged with their fellow actors and the unfolding events of the scene.

Scene Work and Repetition

As actors progress in their training, they begin to apply the principles of the Meisner Technique to more complex scene work. They learn to analyze the given circumstances of the scene, identify their character's objectives and obstacles, and make specific choices to achieve their goals.

Repetition continues to be an important tool in scene work, as actors use it to explore the dynamics of their relationships and uncover deeper emotional truths. Through repetition, actors discover new layers of their characters and develop a greater understanding of the scene's dramatic tension.

The Meisner Technique in Practice

The Meisner Technique is widely taught in acting schools and studios around the world. Actors who study this technique often find it transformative, as it challenges them to be fully present and emotionally available in their performances.

The Meisner Technique is not a quick fix or a shortcut to success in acting. It requires dedication, discipline, and a willingness to explore the depths of one's emotions. However, for those who commit to the process, the Meisner Technique offers a powerful and effective approach to creating truthful and compelling performances.

In conclusion, the Meisner Technique is a renowned method of acting that emphasizes the actor's ability to respond truthfully in the present moment. Through exercises such as repetition, emotional preparation, and active listening, actors develop a deep connection to their characters and their fellow performers. The Meisner Technique offers a valuable tool for actors seeking to create authentic and engaging performances.

CHAPTER 9

THE METHOD ACTING APPROACH

Method acting is a widely recognized and influential approach to acting that has had a significant impact on the craft. Developed by Constantin Stanislavski and popularized by actors such as Marlon Brando, James Dean, and Robert De Niro, the Method Acting Approach emphasizes the use of personal experiences and emotions to create authentic and believable performances.

The Origins of Method Acting

The roots of Method acting can be traced back to the early 20th century and the work of Russian theater practitioner Constantin Stanislavski. Stanislavski sought to create a more realistic and naturalistic style of acting that would resonate with audiences on a deeper level. He believed that actors should draw from their own personal experiences and emotions to bring truth and authenticity to their performances.

Stanislavski's teachings were further developed and expanded upon by his students, most notably Lee Strasberg, who went on to establish the Group Theatre in New York City. Strasberg refined and popularized Stanislavski's techniques, which eventually became known as the Method.

The Core Principles of Method Acting

At the heart of the Method Acting Approach are several core principles that guide actors in their pursuit of truth and authenticity in their performances:

Emotional Memory: Method actors rely on their own personal experiences and memories to tap into the emotions required for a particular scene or character. By recalling past experiences that evoke similar emotions, actors can create a genuine emotional connection to their characters.

Sense Memory: Method actors also utilize their senses to recreate the physical and emotional sensations associated with a particular experience. By engaging their senses, actors can fully immerse themselves in the moment and bring a heightened level of realism to their performances.

Substitution: Method actors often use substitution as a technique to connect with their characters. They may substitute their own personal experiences or emotions with those of their characters, allowing them to empathize and understand their motivations and behaviors

Given Circumstances: Method actors pay close attention to the given circumstances of a scene or character. They explore the character's background, relationships, and environment to fully understand the context in which their character exists. This understanding helps them make informed choices and bring depth to their performances.

Physicality and Vocalization: Method actors believe that physicality and vocalization are essential components of a character's portrayal. They pay attention to their body language, gestures, and vocal tone to convey the inner life of their characters.

The Intensity of Method Acting

One of the distinguishing features of Method acting is its emphasis on emotional intensity. Method actors are known for fully immersing themselves in their characters, often blurring the lines between their personal and professional lives. They are willing to go to great lengths to achieve the emotional truth required for a role, sometimes pushing themselves to the brink of their own emotional limits.

This level of intensity can be both rewarding and challenging for actors. On one hand, it allows for deeply nuanced and powerful performances that resonate with audiences. On the other hand, it can take a toll on an actor's emotional well-being if not managed properly. It is crucial for Method actors to have a support system in place and to engage in self-care practices to maintain their emotional balance.

The Impact of Method Acting

Method acting has had a profound influence on the acting profession and has shaped the way actors approach their craft. It has challenged traditional notions of performance and encouraged a more naturalistic and emotionally grounded style of acting.

The Method has also influenced other acting techniques and approaches, such as the Meisner Technique and the Strasberg Method. Many contemporary actors continue to draw inspiration from the principles of Method acting, adapting and incorporating them into their own unique approaches.

Criticisms and Controversies

While Method acting has garnered immense respect and admiration, it has also faced criticism and controversy. Some argue that the intense emotional immersion required by Method acting can lead to unhealthy and potentially dangerous practices. Others believe that it can hinder an actor's ability to separate themselves from their characters, leading to difficulties in their personal lives.

It is important to note that Method acting is not the only valid approach to acting. Different actors may resonate with different techniques, and what works for one may not work for another. Ultimately, the choice of acting method is a personal one, and actors should explore and experiment with various approaches to find what best serves their craft.

In conclusion, the Method Acting Approach is a powerful and influential technique that emphasizes emotional truth and authenticity in performances. It has revolutionized the acting profession and continues to shape the way actors approach their craft. While it may not be suitable for every actor or every role, its principles and teachings have left an indelible mark on the art of acting.

CHAPTER 10
THE BRECHTIAN APPROACH

The Brechtian approach to acting is a unique and influential method that was developed by German playwright and director, Bertolt Brecht. Brecht believed that traditional forms of theater, which aimed to create an emotional connection between the audience and the characters, were ineffective in promoting social and political change. Instead, he sought to create a more critical and analytical form of theater that would encourage the audience to think and question the world around them.

The Origins of the Brechtian Approach

Bertolt Brecht was a highly influential figure in 20th-century theater. He believed that theater should not simply entertain, but also educate and provoke thought. Brecht's approach to acting was heavily influenced by his Marxist beliefs and his desire to expose the social and political injustices of his time. He wanted to create a theater that would challenge the audience's preconceived notions and encourage them to actively engage with the performance.

Key Principles of the Brechtian Approach

The Brechtian approach to acting is characterized by several key principles that set it apart from other methods:

Verfremdungseffekt (Alienation Effect): One of the central concepts of the Brechtian approach is the idea of alienating the audience from the performance. Brecht believed that by breaking the illusion of reality, the audience would be able to critically engage with the play. Actors are encouraged to use techniques such as direct address, exaggerated gestures, and self-conscious acting to remind the audience that they are watching a performance.

Historification: Brecht believed that theater should not be set in a timeless and abstract world, but rather rooted in a specific historical and social context. By presenting the play as a reflection of a particular time and place, the audience is encouraged to draw connections between the events on stage and the world they live in.

Gestus: Brecht emphasized the importance of physical gestures and movements in conveying meaning. Actors are encouraged to use exaggerated and stylized gestures to communicate the social and political attitudes of their characters. This helps to distance the audience from the characters and encourages them to analyze the actions and motivations of the characters.

Epic Theater: Brecht's approach to theater is often referred to as "epic theater" because it aims to present a series of episodic scenes rather than a continuous narrative. This fragmentation of the story allows the audience to critically analyze each scene and draw their own conclusions.

Didacticism: Unlike traditional theater, which aims to entertain, the Brechtian approach is didactic in nature. Brecht wanted to use theater as a means of educating the audience and promoting social and political change. His plays often included explicit messages and moral lessons.

Techniques Used in the Brechtian Approach

To achieve the desired effect, actors using the Brechtian approach employ a range of techniques:

Breaking the Fourth Wall: Actors directly address the audience, acknowledging their presence and reminding them that they are watching a performance. This breaks the illusion of reality and encourages the audience to critically engage with the play.

Exaggerated Gestures and Movements: Actors use exaggerated and stylized gestures to convey meaning. These gestures are often larger than life and help to distance the audience from the characters, encouraging them to analyze the actions and motivations of the characters.

Verbal Gestures: Actors use their voices to emphasize the social and political attitudes of their characters. They may use a range of vocal techniques, such as changing pitch, volume, and rhythm, to convey meaning.

Tableau: Actors freeze in a specific pose or tableau to highlight a particular moment or image. This technique allows the audience to reflect on the scene and draw their own conclusions.

Montage: Brecht often used montage techniques in his plays, where scenes are juxtaposed to create a specific effect. This technique encourages the audience to make connections between seemingly unrelated events and ideas.

Impact and Legacy of the Brechtian Approach

The Brechtian approach to acting has had a profound impact on theater and performance art. Brecht's emphasis on critical thinking, social commentary, and audience engagement has influenced generations of actors, directors, and playwrights. His techniques have been adapted and incorporated into various forms of theater, including political theater, documentary theater, and experimental theater.

The Brechtian approach continues to be relevant today, as it challenges traditional notions of theater and encourages audiences to question the world around them. By breaking the illusion of reality and promoting critical engagement, the Brechtian approach has the power to inspire social and political change through the medium of theater.

PART FOUR

MYTHS AND MISCONCEPTIONS ABOUT ACTING

CHAPTER 11

ACTING IS JUST PRETENDING

Acting is often misunderstood as simply pretending or playing make-believe. However, this misconception fails to capture the true essence and complexity of the craft. Acting is an art form that requires skill, technique, and a deep understanding of human emotions and behavior. In this section, we will debunk the myth that acting is just pretending and explore the depth and intricacies of the actor's craft.

At its core, acting is about embodying a character and bringing them to life in a believable and authentic way. It goes beyond mere imitation or mimicry; it involves delving into the character's psyche, motivations, and emotions. Actors strive to create a connection between themselves and the character they are portraying, allowing the audience to suspend their disbelief and become fully immersed in the story.

To achieve this level of authenticity, actors employ a range of techniques and tools. They study the script, analyze the character's background and relationships, and explore their emotional journey throughout the story. They develop a deep understanding of the character's desires, fears, and conflicts, allowing them to portray a fully realized and multidimensional individual.

Acting also requires a keen sense of observation and empathy. Actors observe and study human behavior, both in themselves and in others, to accurately portray a wide range of emotions and experiences. They tap into their own emotional reservoirs and draw upon personal experiences to bring truth and depth to their performances.

Furthermore, acting involves a mastery of physicality and vocal expression. Actors use their bodies and voices as instruments to convey the character's physicality, gestures, and vocal nuances. They pay attention to their posture, movement, and vocal tone to create a believable and compelling portrayal.

Acting is not just about pretending to be someone else; it is about exploring the human condition and illuminating universal truths. Through their performances, actors have the power to evoke empathy, provoke thought, and inspire change. They have the ability to shed light on different perspectives, challenge societal norms, and create a deeper understanding of the human experience.

Actors also collaborate closely with directors, fellow actors, and other members of the production team to bring a story to life. They work together to create a cohesive and harmonious performance that engages and captivates the audience. This collaborative process requires a high level of professionalism, adaptability, and teamwork.

Contrary to popular belief, acting is not an easy profession. It demands dedication, discipline, and continuous learning. Actors invest countless hours in honing their craft and attending acting classes, workshops, and rehearsals. They constantly seek opportunities to expand their skill set, challenge themselves, and grow as artists.

Acting also requires a strong emotional resilience. Actors often face rejection, criticism, and the pressure to perform under challenging circumstances. They must learn to navigate these obstacles while maintaining their emotional well-being and staying true to their artistic vision.

In conclusion, acting is far more than just pretending. It is a complex and multifaceted art form that requires skill, technique, and a deep understanding of human nature. Actors strive to create authentic and compelling performances that resonate with audiences on a profound level. They are storytellers, truth-seekers, and catalysts for change. So, the next time you watch a film or attend a play, remember that the actors on stage or screen are not merely pretending; they are artists dedicated to their craft, bringing characters and stories to life in a way that touches our hearts and minds.

CHAPTER 12
ACTORS ARE BORN, NOT MADE

One of the most common myths about acting is the belief that actors are born with a natural talent and cannot be made through training and practice. This misconception often leads to the assumption that only a select few individuals possess the innate ability to become successful actors. However, this notion is far from the truth. While it is true that some individuals may have a natural inclination towards acting, the idea that talent alone is enough to succeed in the field is misleading. Acting is a craft that requires dedication, hard work, and continuous learning. Just like any other skill, acting can be developed and honed through training, practice, and experience.

One of the most renowned acting methods is the Stanislavski System, developed by Russian actor and director Konstantin Stanislavski. This approach emphasizes the importance of psychological realism and the actor's ability to create believable characters by tapping into their own emotions and experiences. The Stanislavski System provides actors with a set of tools and techniques to explore their characters' motivations, objectives, and inner lives.

Another influential acting technique is the Meisner Technique, developed by American actor and teacher Sanford Meisner. This approach focuses on truthful and spontaneous reactions by encouraging actors to fully immerse themselves in the present moment and respond honestly to their scene partners. The Meisner Technique helps actors develop their listening skills, emotional responsiveness, and the ability to live truthfully under imaginary circumstances.

The Method Acting approach, popularized by actors such as Marlon Brando and Robert De Niro, involves the actor drawing from their own personal experiences and emotions to create authentic and deeply layered performances. This technique encourages actors to fully embody their characters both physically and emotionally, often requiring extensive research and preparation.

The Brechtian Approach, developed by German playwright and director Bertolt Brecht, focuses on creating a sense of distance between the actor and the character, allowing the audience to critically engage with the performance. This technique emphasizes the use of theatrical devices, such as breaking the fourth wall and employing alienation techniques, to provoke social and political awareness.

These are just a few examples of the many acting methods and techniques that actors can study and utilize to enhance their craft. Each approach offers a unique perspective and set of tools for actors to explore and incorporate into their performances. By studying and practicing these methods, actors can develop their skills, expand their range, and become more versatile performers.

Furthermore, acting training goes beyond just learning specific techniques. It also involves developing a deep understanding of storytelling, character analysis, vocal and physical techniques, improvisation, and stage presence. Acting classes and workshops provide a structured environment for actors to learn and practice these skills under the guidance of experienced instructors.

It is important to remember that acting is not a static skill. It is a lifelong journey of growth and development. Even the most talented actors continue to learn and evolve throughout their careers. They constantly seek new challenges, take on diverse roles, and push themselves outside of their comfort zones.

In conclusion, the belief that actors are born, not made, is a myth that undermines the hard work and dedication that goes into becoming a skilled actor. While some individuals may have a natural inclination towards acting, anyone with a passion for the craft can develop their skills through training, practice, and experience. Acting is a craft that can be learned, honed, and continuously improved upon. With the right mindset, commitment, and willingness to learn, anyone can pursue a successful career in acting.

CHAPTER 13
ACTING IS EASY

Acting is often perceived as an effortless and glamorous profession. Many people believe that actors simply memorize lines and play pretend, making it seem like an easy job. However, this is far from the truth. Acting is a complex and demanding craft that requires dedication, skill, and hard work. In this section, we will debunk the myth that acting is easy and explore the challenges and complexities that actors face.

The Illusion of Effortlessness

One of the reasons why people may think that acting is easy is because actors make their performances appear effortless. Skilled actors have the ability to fully immerse themselves in a character, making it seem like they are not acting at all. This illusion of effortlessness is a testament to their talent and training.

However, behind the scenes, actors put in countless hours of preparation and practice to achieve this level of authenticity. They undergo extensive training to develop their craft, studying various acting techniques, honing their emotional range, and perfecting their physicality. They also spend time researching and analyzing their characters, understanding their motivations, and creating a believable backstory. All of this work happens before they even step foot on stage or in front of a camera.

Emotional and Psychological Demands

Acting requires actors to tap into a wide range of emotions and portray them convincingly. They must be able to access their own emotions and channel them into their characters, often reliving past experiences or imagining intense situations. This emotional vulnerability can be mentally and psychologically challenging.

Furthermore, actors often have to portray characters with complex and conflicting emotions. They must be able to switch between different emotional states seamlessly and authentically. This requires a deep understanding of human psychology and the ability to empathize with a wide range of experiences.

Physical Demands

Acting is not just about delivering lines; it also involves physicality and movement. Actors must be able to use their bodies to express emotions, convey meaning, and create dynamic performances. They need to have control over their gestures, facial expressions, and body language to effectively communicate with the audience.

In addition, actors may be required to perform physically demanding scenes, such as fight sequences or dance numbers. They must undergo rigorous physical training to develop the strength, flexibility, and stamina necessary to execute these scenes safely and convincingly.

Memorization and Adaptability

Memorizing lines is a fundamental aspect of acting, but it is not as simple as it may seem. Actors must not only memorize their own lines but also be familiar with the entire script to understand the context and dynamics of the scene. They need to be able to recall their lines effortlessly while staying fully present in the moment and responding to their co-actors.

Furthermore, actors must be adaptable and able to adjust their performances based on the director's vision and feedback. They need to be able to take direction and make adjustments on the spot, sometimes even during live performances. This requires quick thinking, flexibility, and the ability to make split-second decisions while staying true to the character.

The Pressure of Performance

Actors often face intense pressure to deliver exceptional performances. Whether it's on stage or in front of a camera, they are constantly being evaluated and critiqued. They must be able to handle this pressure and perform consistently, even under challenging circumstances.

Additionally, actors often work long hours, sometimes in demanding environments. They may have to shoot scenes repeatedly, perform in front of large audiences, or work in extreme weather conditions. This can take a toll on their physical and mental well-being, requiring them to maintain a high level of focus and energy throughout the production.

Conclusion

Acting is far from easy. It is a demanding and multifaceted profession that requires a combination of talent, training, and hard work. Actors must possess a deep understanding of human emotions, physicality, and storytelling. They must be able to adapt to different roles, memorize lines, and perform under pressure. While acting may appear effortless on the surface, it is the result of countless hours of preparation, dedication, and a lifelong commitment to the craft. So, the next time you watch a performance, remember that behind the scenes, there is a talented actor who has put in a tremendous amount of effort to make it look easy.

CHAPTER 14
ACTING IS NOT A REAL JOB

Acting is often misunderstood and undervalued as a profession. Many people believe that acting is not a real job, but rather a hobby or a form of entertainment. However, this misconception couldn't be further from the truth. Acting is a legitimate and demanding profession that requires skill, dedication, and hard work.

One of the reasons why some people may view acting as not being a real job is because it is often associated with fame and glamour. The media often portrays actors as living a luxurious lifestyle, attending red-carpet events, and receiving hefty paychecks. While it is true that some actors achieve fame and fortune, the reality is that the majority of actors struggle to make a living from their craft.

Acting is a highly competitive field, and only a small percentage of actors achieve financial success. Many actors work long hours, often juggling multiple jobs to make ends meet. They face constant rejection and uncertainty, as they navigate auditions, callbacks, and the casting process. Acting requires a significant investment of time, energy, and resources, including training, headshots, and travel expenses.

Furthermore, acting is not just about memorizing lines and delivering them convincingly. It involves a deep understanding of human emotions, psychology, and storytelling. Actors must be able to connect with their characters on a profound level, bringing them to life in a way that is authentic and compelling. They must possess the ability to portray a wide range of emotions, often in challenging and emotionally demanding situations.

Actors also need to have a strong physical presence and be able to use their bodies effectively to convey meaning and communicate with the audience. They must be skilled in movement and have a keen sense of spatial awareness. Voice and diction are also crucial aspects of acting, as actors need to be able to project their voices and articulate their words clearly, whether on stage or in front of a camera.

In addition to the artistic and technical skills required, acting also demands a high level of professionalism and discipline. Actors must be punctual, reliable, and able to work well with others. They need to be adaptable and able to take direction from directors and collaborate effectively with their co-actors. Acting is a team effort, and actors must be able to work together to create a cohesive and compelling performance.

Actors also play a vital role in society. They have the power to inspire, educate, and provoke thought through their performances. They bring stories to life, shedding light on different perspectives and experiences. Acting has the ability to challenge societal norms, break down barriers, and promote empathy and understanding.

Moreover, acting is not limited to just one medium. Actors can work in theater, film, television, commercials, voice-over work, and more. Each medium presents its own unique challenges and opportunities, requiring actors to adapt their skills and techniques accordingly. This versatility and adaptability make acting a dynamic and ever-evolving profession.

PART FIVE

PREPARING FOR A ROLE

CHAPTER 15
SCRIPT ANALYSIS

Script analysis is a crucial step in the preparation process for any actor. It involves a thorough examination and understanding of the script, its characters, themes, and overall structure. By dissecting the script, actors can gain valuable insights that will inform their performance and help them bring the story to life on stage or screen.

The Importance of Script Analysis

Script analysis is the foundation upon which a successful performance is built. It allows actors to fully grasp the intentions of the playwright or screenwriter and interpret their words in a meaningful way. By understanding the script's structure, themes, and character arcs, actors can make informed choices about their performance and create a more authentic and compelling portrayal.

One of the primary goals of script analysis is to identify the given circumstances of the play or film. This includes understanding the time period, location, social context, and relationships between characters. By immersing themselves in the world of the script, actors can better understand the motivations and behaviors of their characters.

Steps in Script Analysis

Read the script multiple times: The first step in script analysis is to read the script thoroughly. It is essential to read it multiple times to gain a deeper understanding of the story, characters, and dialogue. Each reading will reveal new layers and nuances that may have been missed initially.

Identify the main themes: Analyze the script to identify the main themes and ideas that the playwright or screenwriter is exploring. This will help actors connect with the underlying messages of the story and convey them effectively to the audience.

Break down the structure: Examine the structure of the script, including acts, scenes, and beats. Identify the major turning points, conflicts, and resolutions. Understanding the structure will help actors navigate the emotional journey of their characters and create a cohesive performance.

Analyze the characters: Dive deep into the characters' backgrounds, motivations, and relationships. Identify their objectives, obstacles, and transformations throughout the story. This will enable actors to develop a well-rounded and believable portrayal.

Study the dialogue: Pay close attention to the dialogue and subtext. Look for clues about the characters' emotions, intentions, and hidden meanings. Analyzing the dialogue will help actors deliver their lines with authenticity and depth.

Consider the physical and visual elements: Take note of any physical or visual elements described in the script, such as props, costumes, and set design. These details can provide valuable insights into the world of the play or film and inform the actor's choices.

Research and gather information: Conduct research to enhance your understanding of the script's context. This may involve studying the time period, historical events, or cultural references mentioned in the script. Gathering information will help actors bring a sense of authenticity to their performance.

Applying Script Analysis to Character Development

Script analysis is closely tied to character development. By thoroughly analyzing the script, actors can make informed choices about their characters' objectives, obstacles, and relationships. Here are some ways in which script analysis can inform character development:

Understanding the character's journey: By analyzing the script's structure, actors can identify the key moments in their character's journey. This includes their initial situation, conflicts, and eventual transformation. Understanding this journey will help actors create a well-rounded and dynamic portrayal.

Identifying the character's objectives: Script analysis allows actors to identify their character's objectives in each scene and throughout the story. This understanding helps actors make choices that align with their character's desires and motivations.

Exploring relationships: By analyzing the script's dialogue and stage directions, actors can gain insights into their character's relationships with other characters. This understanding will inform their interactions and dynamics on stage or screen.

Uncovering subtext: Script analysis helps actors uncover the subtext of the dialogue. By understanding what is not explicitly stated, actors can bring depth and complexity to their performance.

Finding physicality and mannerisms: Script analysis can provide clues about a character's physicality, mannerisms, and gestures. By paying attention to these details, actors can create a physicality that is consistent with their character's personality and background.

In conclusion, script analysis is an essential tool for actors in preparing for a role. By thoroughly examining the script, and understanding its structure, themes, and characters, actors can make informed choices that bring depth and authenticity to their performance. Script analysis is the foundation upon which a successful portrayal is built, allowing actors to fully understand and embody their characters.

CHAPTER 16
RESEARCH AND BACKGROUND

Research and background work are essential components of the actor's preparation process. Before stepping into a role, actors must delve into the world of the character they are portraying. This involves conducting thorough research and building a solid foundation of knowledge about the character's background, circumstances, and the world they inhabit. By immersing themselves in this research, actors can bring depth, authenticity, and believability to their performances.

Understanding the Character

To effectively portray a character, actors must first understand who they are portraying. This requires a deep exploration of the character's history, personality, motivations, and relationships. By understanding the character's past experiences, actors can gain insight into their present behavior and make informed choices about how to bring them to life.

Researching the character's background involves studying the script, analyzing the character's dialogue and actions, and identifying any clues or hints provided by the playwright or screenwriter. Actors may also consult with the director, if available, to gain additional insights into the character's intentions and objectives.

Historical and Cultural Context

In addition to understanding the character, actors must also familiarize themselves with the historical and cultural context in which the story takes place. This includes researching the time period, social norms, customs, and traditions relevant to the character and their environment. By gaining a deeper understanding of the historical and cultural context, actors can accurately portray the character's beliefs, values, and mannerisms.

Researching the historical and cultural context may involve reading books, and articles, or watching documentaries about the time period. It may also involve studying photographs, paintings, or other visual references to gain a visual understanding of the setting and the people who inhabited it.

Psychological and Emotional Exploration

To fully embody a character, actors must also explore the character's psychological and emotional makeup. This involves delving into the character's thoughts, feelings, fears, and desires. By understanding the character's inner world, actors can tap into their emotions and portray them authentically on stage or screen.

Psychological and emotional exploration may involve studying psychology, human behavior, and emotional dynamics. Actors may also draw from their own personal experiences and emotions to connect with the character on a deeper level. This process requires introspection, empathy, and a willingness to explore the depths of human emotion.

Physicality and Movement

Researching and developing the physicality and movement of a character is another crucial aspect of an actor's preparation. This involves understanding the character's posture, gestures, mannerisms, and overall physical presence. By embodying the character physically, actors can bring a sense of authenticity and believability to their performances.

To develop the physicality of a character, actors may study movement techniques such as Laban, Alexander Technique, or Viewpoints. They may also observe and study people in real life or watch videos to gain inspiration and insights into different physicalities. By experimenting with different physical choices, actors can find the most effective way to express the character's personality and emotions through their body.

Environmental Research

In some cases, actors may need to research specific environments or professions related to their character. This could involve visiting locations, interviewing experts, or immersing themselves in the world of the character. By gaining firsthand knowledge of the character's environment, actors can bring a sense of authenticity and realism to their performances.

For example, if a character is a doctor, the actor may shadow a real doctor or consult with medical professionals to understand the intricacies of the profession. If a character is from a different country or culture, the actor may engage with individuals from that culture or study their language, customs, and traditions. This level of research helps actors accurately portray the character's world and create a more immersive experience for the audience.

Collaboration with the Creative Team

Research and background work are not solely the responsibility of the actor. It is a collaborative process that involves the entire creative team, including the director, costume designer, set designer, and others. By sharing research findings and insights, the team can work together to create a cohesive and authentic world for the characters to inhabit.

Collaboration with the creative team also allows actors to gain different perspectives and interpretations of the character and their world. This exchange of ideas and knowledge enhances the overall quality of the production and ensures that all elements align with the director's vision.

In conclusion, research and background work are vital components of an actor's preparation process. By understanding the character, exploring the historical and cultural context, delving into the character's psychology and emotions, developing the physicality, and conducting environmental research, actors can bring depth, authenticity, and believability to their performances. This thorough preparation not only enhances the actor's understanding of the character but also enriches the overall storytelling experience for the audience.

CHAPTER 17
CREATING A CHARACTER

Creating a character is a fundamental aspect of acting. It involves developing a deep understanding of the character's background, motivations, and personality traits in order to bring them to life on stage or screen. This process requires careful analysis, research, and imagination to fully embody the character and make them believable to the audience. In this section, we will explore the various techniques and approaches actors use to create compelling and authentic characters.

Understanding the Script

Before diving into the process of creating a character, it is essential to thoroughly understand the script. This involves reading and analyzing the text to gain insights into the character's relationships, objectives, conflicts, and overall journey throughout the story. By understanding the context and the character's place within the narrative, actors can make informed choices about how to portray them.

Research and Observation

Once the script has been thoroughly understood, actors often engage in research and observation to enhance their understanding of the character. This may involve studying similar real-life individuals, historical figures, or even fictional characters that share similarities with the role they are portraying. By observing their behavior, mannerisms, speech patterns, and physicality, actors can add depth and authenticity to their portrayal.

Building a Backstory

Creating a backstory for the character is another crucial step in the process of character development. This involves imagining the character's past experiences, relationships, and events that have shaped their personality and motivations. By delving into their history, actors can better understand why the character behaves the way they do and make more informed choices about their actions and reactions.

Physicality and Movement

Physicality plays a significant role in bringing a character to life. Actors must consider how their character moves, stands, and gestures, as these physical attributes can reveal a great deal about their personality and emotional state. By experimenting with different physical choices, actors can find the most effective way to embody their characters physically.

Physicality and Movement

Physicality plays a significant role in bringing a character to life. Actors must consider how their character moves, stands, and gestures, as these physical attributes can reveal a great deal about their personality and emotional state. By experimenting with different physical choices, actors can find the most effective way to embody their characters physically.

Voice and Speech

Just as physicality is important, so is the character's voice and speech. Actors must consider the character's accent, tone, pitch, and rhythm of speech to accurately portray their personality and background. By working with vocal coaches or dialect specialists, actors can develop a unique and authentic voice for their characters.

Emotional Connection

To create a believable character, actors must establish an emotional connection with them. This involves tapping into their own emotions and finding ways to relate to the character's experiences and feelings. By drawing on personal experiences or using techniques such as sense memory, actors can access the necessary emotions to bring their characters to life.

Collaboration with the Director

Creating a character is not solely the responsibility of the actor. Collaboration with the director is crucial in shaping and refining the portrayal. Directors provide guidance and feedback, helping actors to fine-tune their performance and ensure it aligns with the overall vision of the production. Through open communication and a willingness to explore different ideas, actors, and directors can work together to create a fully realized character.

Rehearsal Process

The rehearsal process is where actors have the opportunity to experiment, refine, and fully embody their character. Through scene work, improvisation, and discussions with fellow actors, the character begins to take shape and evolve. Rehearsals allow actors to explore different choices, discover nuances, and develop a deeper understanding of their character's motivations and relationships.

Continual Exploration

Creating a character is an ongoing process that continues throughout the entire production. As actors delve deeper into their characters, they may uncover new layers and insights that inform their performance. It is essential to remain open to exploration and be willing to adapt and grow as the character develops.

In conclusion, creating a character is a multifaceted process that requires a combination of analysis, research, imagination, and collaboration. By understanding the script, conducting research, building a backstory, exploring physicality and voice, establishing an emotional connection, collaborating with the director, and engaging in the rehearsal process, actors can create compelling and authentic characters that resonate with audiences. The journey of creating a character is a deeply rewarding and transformative experience for actors, allowing them to step into the shoes of another person and bring their story to life.

CHAPTER 18
REHEARSAL TECHNIQUES

Rehearsal is a crucial part of the acting process. It is during this time that actors have the opportunity to explore their characters, develop their relationships with other actors, and refine their performances. Rehearsals allow actors to experiment, make mistakes, and ultimately find the truth in their characters and the story they are telling. In this section, we will explore some effective rehearsal techniques that actors can use to enhance their performances.

TableWork: Tablework is a rehearsal technique that involves sitting around a table with the director and the rest of the cast to analyze the script and discuss the characters, themes, and overall vision of the production. This technique allows actors to gain a deeper understanding of the story and their characters' motivations. During table work, actors can ask questions, share insights, and collaborate with the director and fellow cast members to ensure a cohesive interpretation of the script.

Line Memorization: Before diving into the emotional and physical aspects of a character, it is essential for actors to have their lines memorized. Line memorization allows actors to focus on the nuances of their performance without the distraction of trying to remember their dialogue. There are various techniques actors can use to memorize lines, such as repetition, writing them down, or recording themselves and listening to the lines repeatedly. The key is to find a method that works best for each individual actor.

Character Exploration: During rehearsals, actors have the opportunity to delve deep into their characters and explore their motivations, desires, and fears. One effective technique for character exploration is the "four W's" - who, what, where, and why. Actors ask themselves questions about their characters, such as who they are, what they want, where they come from, and why they behave the way they do. By answering these questions, actors can develop a rich and multi-dimensional portrayal of their characters.

Improvisation

Improvisation is a valuable rehearsal technique that allows actors to think on their feet and explore different possibilities within a scene. By improvising, actors can discover new insights about their characters and the relationships between them. Improvisation also helps actors to be present in the moment and respond authentically to their fellow actors. This technique can be particularly useful when working on scenes with complex emotions or when exploring different choices for a character's actions.

Blocking

Blocking refers to the movement and positioning of actors on stage or on camera. During rehearsals, directors and actors work together to determine the blocking for each scene. This includes where actors enter and exit, where they stand or sit, and how they move throughout the space. Blocking is essential for creating visually interesting and dynamic scenes. It also helps actors to understand the physicality of their characters and how their movements contribute to the overall storytelling.

Scene Analysis

Scene analysis involves breaking down a scene into its essential components, such as the objectives, obstacles, and tactics of each character. By analyzing the scene, actors can gain a deeper understanding of the dynamics at play and make informed choices about their performances. Scene analysis also helps actors identify the beats and transitions within a scene, allowing for a more nuanced and compelling portrayal.

Emotional Preparation

Acting often requires tapping into deep emotions and portraying them authentically. Emotional preparation is a rehearsal technique that helps actors access and channel their emotions effectively. This can involve personalizing the character's experiences, recalling past memories, or using sensory exercises to evoke specific emotions. Emotional preparation allows actors to connect with their characters on a deeper level and bring truth and depth to their performances.

Run-throughs

Run-throughs are full rehearsals of the entire play or scene from start to finish. This technique allows actors to experience the flow and pacing of the production and identify any areas that need improvement. Run-throughs also help actors to build stamina and develop a sense of ensemble with their fellow cast members. It is during run-throughs that actors can refine their performances, make adjustments, and ensure that the production is cohesive and engaging.

Feedback and Collaboration

Rehearsals are a collaborative process, and feedback plays a vital role in the development of performance. Actors should be open to receiving feedback from the director and their fellow cast members. Constructive criticism can help actors refine their performances, discover new insights, and make necessary adjustments. Collaboration is key during rehearsals, as actors work together to create a cohesive and compelling production.

Reflection and Revision

Throughout the rehearsal process, actors should take time for reflection and revision. This involves reviewing their performances, identifying areas for improvement, and making necessary adjustments. Actors can also seek feedback from trusted mentors or acting coaches to gain fresh perspectives on their work. Reflection and revision allow actors to continually grow and refine their performances, ensuring that they deliver their best work on stage or on screen

PART SIX

ACTING FOR DIFFERENT MEDIUMS

CHAPTER 19
STAGE ACTING

Stage acting is a unique and exhilarating form of acting that requires a specific set of skills and techniques. Unlike film or television acting, stage acting involves performing live in front of an audience, which adds an extra layer of challenge and excitement to the craft. In this section, we will explore the intricacies of stage acting, including the importance of projection, physicality, and connecting with the audience.

The Power of Projection

One of the key aspects of stage acting is the ability to project your voice and emotions to reach every corner of the theater. Unlike in film or television, where microphones and close-up shots can capture subtle nuances, stage actors must rely on their vocal projection to ensure that their performance is heard and understood by the entire audience.

To effectively project your voice, it is essential to use proper breath control and vocal techniques. This includes diaphragmatic breathing, which allows you to generate enough air to support your voice and project it with clarity and volume. Additionally, articulation and diction play a crucial role in ensuring that your words are intelligible to the audience, even in large theaters.

Physicality and Movement

Stage acting also requires a heightened sense of physicality and movement. Unlike in film or television, where the camera can capture close-ups and subtle gestures, stage actors must use their entire body to convey emotions and tell a story. Every movement, gesture, and facial expression must be exaggerated to ensure that it reaches the back of the theater.

Physicality in stage acting involves understanding and utilizing the space on the stage effectively. This includes blocking, which refers to the planned movement and positioning of actors on stage. Blocking helps create visually appealing compositions and ensures that the audience can see and follow the action.

In addition to blocking, stage actors must also be aware of their body language and posture. Every movement should be purposeful and intentional, contributing to the overall storytelling. Physicality can also be used to differentiate characters and convey their personalities, adding depth and dimension to the performance.

Connecting with the Audience

One of the most rewarding aspects of stage acting is the direct connection with the audience. Unlike in film or television, where actors are separated from the viewers by a screen, stage actors can see and feel the immediate reactions of the audience. This interaction creates a unique energy and allows for a dynamic exchange between the performers and the spectators.

The Importance of Rehearsal

Stage acting requires extensive rehearsal to ensure a seamless and polished performance. Rehearsals allow actors to familiarize themselves with the script, develop their characters, and work on blocking and timing. It is during rehearsals that actors can experiment, make choices, and collaborate with the director and fellow cast members.

Rehearsals also provide an opportunity for actors to build chemistry and develop a cohesive ensemble. Through the process of rehearsing together, actors can establish trust, understand each other's rhythms, and create a sense of unity on stage. This collaboration is essential for a successful stage production.

In addition to the technical aspects of the performance, rehearsals also allow actors to explore the emotional depth of their characters. They can delve into the motivations, conflicts, and relationships within the play, bringing authenticity and depth to their performances.

Adapting to Different Stage Environments

Stage acting can take place in a variety of environments, from small intimate theaters to large auditoriums. Each stage environment presents its own set of challenges and requires actors to adapt their performances accordingly.

In smaller theaters, actors may need to tone down their physicality and vocal projection to maintain a sense of intimacy. On the other hand, in larger venues, actors must amplify their movements and voices to ensure that their performance reaches the entire audience.

Stage actors must also be adaptable to different stage configurations and set designs. They must be able to navigate and utilize the space effectively, making the most of the available props, set pieces, and stage entrances and exits.

Conclusion

Stage acting is a thrilling and demanding form of acting that requires a unique set of skills. From projecting their voice to utilizing physicality and connecting with the audience, stage actors must master various techniques to deliver a compelling performance. Through extensive rehearsal and adaptability, stage actors can bring stories to life and create memorable experiences for both themselves and the audience.

CHAPTER 20
FILM ACTING

Film acting is a unique and specialized form of acting that requires a different set of skills and techniques compared to stage acting. While both mediums involve portraying characters and telling stories, film acting has its own set of challenges and considerations. In this section, we will explore the world of film acting and discuss the methods and techniques that can help actors excel in this medium.

The Camera as a Close Observer

One of the key differences between stage acting and film acting is the presence of the camera. Unlike the stage, where actors must project their voices and movements to reach the entire audience, the camera in the film captures every subtle nuance and detail of an actor's performance. This means that film actors must learn to work with the camera as their closest observer.

Film actors need to be aware of their physicality, facial expressions, and even the smallest gestures, as these can be magnified on screen. The camera can capture the tiniest flicker of emotion in an actor's eyes or the subtlest change in their body language. Therefore, film actors must develop a heightened sense of self-awareness and control over their physicality to ensure that their performances translate effectively on screen.

Naturalism and Authenticity

Film acting often requires a more naturalistic and realistic approach compared to stage acting. The intimacy of the camera allows for a more nuanced and subtle portrayal of emotions and characters. Film actors must strive for authenticity in their performances, creating characters that feel genuine and relatable to the audience.

To achieve this, film actors often rely on internalization and emotional truth. They delve deep into their characters' motivations, emotions, and experiences, and bring them to life in a way that feels authentic. This requires a deep understanding of the character's backstory, psychology, and relationships, allowing the actor to embody the character fully.

Adaptability and Flexibility

Film actors must be adaptable and flexible in their approach to acting. Unlike stage actors who have the luxury of performing a scene from start to finish in one take, film actors often work in small segments or "takes." They must be able to maintain consistency in their performance across multiple takes, even if the scenes are shot out of order.

Technical Considerations

Film acting also involves understanding and navigating various technical aspects of the filmmaking process. Actors must be aware of camera angles, lighting, and blocking, as these elements can greatly impact their performances. They need to know how to position themselves in relation to the camera, how to use their bodies and voices to create the desired effect, and how to work within the constraints of the film set.

Additionally, film actors must be comfortable with the concept of "hitting their marks." This refers to the precise positioning of actors in relation to the camera and other elements of the scene. Hitting marks ensures that actors are in the correct position for the camera to capture their performances effectively. It requires spatial awareness and the ability to move with precision and consistency.

Emotional Stamina and Endurance

Film acting can be physically and emotionally demanding. Actors may be required to perform intense or emotionally charged scenes repeatedly over the course of several hours or days. This requires emotional stamina and the ability to tap into and sustain the necessary emotions for each take.

Film actors must also be able to handle long hours on set, waiting for their scenes to be filmed, and maintaining focus and energy throughout the filming process. They need to take care of their physical and emotional well-being to ensure they can deliver consistent and compelling performances.

In conclusion, film acting is a specialized form of acting that requires a unique set of skills and techniques. Actors must learn to work with the camera as their closest observer, strive for authenticity and naturalism, be adaptable and flexible, understand technical aspects of filmmaking, and have the emotional stamina to sustain their performances. By honing these skills and techniques, actors can excel in the world of film acting and bring their characters to life on the silver screen.

CHAPTER 21 TELEVISION ACTING

Television acting is a unique and challenging form of acting that requires a specific set of skills and techniques. While many of the principles of acting apply across different mediums, there are certain considerations that are specific to television. In this section, we will explore the world of television acting and discuss the methods and approaches that can help actors succeed in this medium

Understanding the Medium

Television acting differs from stage acting and film acting in several ways. One of the key differences is the intimacy of the medium. Television audiences are often watching actors on small screens in their homes, which means that subtle facial expressions and gestures can have a significant impact. Actors must learn to convey emotions and tell stories effectively within the confines of the television screen.

Another important aspect of television acting is the fast-paced nature of the industry. Television shows often have tight shooting schedules, with actors having to deliver their best performances quickly and efficiently. This requires actors to be adaptable, flexible, and able to make quick adjustments to their performances based on the director's instructions.

Developing Authenticity

One of the challenges of television acting is maintaining authenticity while working within the constraints of the medium. Unlike stage acting, where actors have the luxury of projecting their voices and movements to reach a large audience, television acting requires a more naturalistic approach. Actors must learn to convey emotions and engage the audience through subtle and nuanced performances.

To develop authenticity in television acting, actors can focus on the following techniques:

Internalization: Television actors often have limited rehearsal time, so it is crucial to internalize the character's emotions and motivations. By understanding the character's backstory and objectives, actors can bring depth and authenticity to their performances.

Listening and Reacting: Television acting is not just about delivering lines; it is about actively listening and reacting to other characters. By genuinely listening and responding in the moment, actors can create authentic and believable interactions on screen.

Physicality: While television acting requires a more naturalistic approach, physicality still plays a crucial role. Actors must be aware of their body language and use it to convey emotions and enhance their performances.

Eye Contact: In television, eye contact is essential for creating a connection with the audience. Actors must learn to use their eyes effectively to convey emotions and engage viewers.

Adapting to the Technical Aspects

Television acting also involves understanding and adapting to the technical aspects of the medium. Unlike stage acting, where actors have the freedom to move around a large space, television actors must work within the confines of the camera frame. This requires actors to be aware of their blocking and positioning in relation to the camera.

Collaborating with the Production Team

Television acting is a collaborative process that involves working closely with the production team, including directors, writers, and fellow actors. It is essential for actors to understand and respect the vision of the director while also bringing their own creativity and interpretation to the role.

Communication and collaboration are key in television acting. Actors must be open to feedback and willing to make adjustments based on the director's vision. They should also be proactive in seeking clarification and discussing their character's development with the writers and directors.

Building a Versatile Skill Set

To succeed in television acting, actors must develop a versatile skill set that allows them to adapt to different genres and styles. Television offers a wide range of genres, from drama to comedy, and actors must be able to navigate and excel in each of them.

Actors can enhance their versatility by taking on diverse roles and challenging themselves to explore different characters and genres. They can also benefit from training in improvisation, as television often requires actors to think on their feet and make quick decisions.

Conclusion

Television acting presents unique challenges and opportunities for actors. By understanding the specific requirements of the medium and developing the necessary skills and techniques, actors can thrive in the world of television. Authenticity, adaptability, and collaboration are key to success in television acting, and actors who embrace these principles can create compelling and memorable performances that resonate with audiences.

CHAPTER 22
VOICE ACTING

Voice acting is a specialized form of acting that focuses solely on the use of the voice to bring characters to life. It is a unique and challenging field that requires a different set of skills compared to stage or film acting. In this section, we will explore the world of voice acting, including its techniques, challenges, and rewards.

The Importance of the Voice

In voice acting, the voice becomes the primary tool for conveying emotions, creating characters, and telling stories. Unlike stage or film acting, where physicality and facial expressions play a significant role, voice actors must rely solely on their vocal abilities to captivate and engage the audience. The voice becomes the vehicle through which the character's personality, emotions, and intentions are conveyed.

Developing Vocal Skills

To excel in voice acting, it is crucial to develop a wide range of vocal skills. Here are some key areas to focus on:

Vocal Range and Flexibility: A voice actor should have a versatile vocal range to portray a variety of characters. This includes the ability to modulate pitch, tone, and volume to create different voices and personalities. Practicing vocal exercises, such as scales and vocal warm-ups, can help expand your range and improve flexibility.

Diction and Articulation: Clear diction and precise articulation are essential in voice acting. Every word and syllable must be pronounced accurately to ensure clarity and understanding. Regular practice of tongue twisters and enunciation exercises can help improve diction and articulation skills.

Emotion and Expression: Voice actors must be able to convey a wide range of emotions through their voice alone. They need to master techniques such as inflection, intonation, and emphasis to effectively communicate the character's feelings and intentions. Developing an understanding of emotional nuances and practicing emotional exercises can enhance your ability to express emotions convincingly.

Breathing and Control: Proper breathing techniques are crucial for voice actors to maintain vocal stamina and control. Deep diaphragmatic breathing allows for sustained projection and prevents vocal strain. Regular breathing exercises and mindfulness practices can help improve breath control and support.

Techniques for Voice Acting

Voice acting requires a different approach compared to other forms of acting. Here are some techniques commonly used by voice actors:

Character Analysis: Before diving into a voice-acting role, it is essential to thoroughly analyze the character. Understand their background, motivations, and personality traits. This analysis will help you make informed choices about how to portray the character through your voice.

Vocal Characterization: Creating distinct and believable character voices is a fundamental skill in voice acting. Experiment with different vocal qualities, accents, and speech patterns to bring the character to life. Practice by recording yourself and listening back to refine your vocal characterization.

Script Interpretation: Voice actors must be skilled at interpreting scripts and understanding the intended tone and emotions. Analyze the script, identify key moments, and make choices about how to deliver the lines effectively. Experiment with pacing, pauses, and emphasis to enhance the impact of the dialogue.

Mic Technique: Working with a microphone is a crucial aspect of voice acting. Understanding proper mic techniques is essential to achieve optimal sound quality and prevent unwanted noise. Learn how to position the microphone correctly, control distance, and modulate volume for different scenes and characters.

Challenges and Rewards of Voice Acting

Voice acting presents its own set of challenges and rewards. Here are a few to consider:

Limited Physicality: Unlike stage or film acting, voice actors do not have the advantage of physical gestures or facial expressions to convey emotions. They must rely solely on their voice, making it essential to develop strong vocal skills and techniques.

Vocal Strain: Voice acting often requires long recording sessions, which can put a strain on the vocal cords. It is crucial to practice proper vocal care, including warm-ups, hydration, and rest, to prevent vocal fatigue and injury.

Versatility: Voice actors are often required to portray a wide range of characters, from young children to elderly individuals, and even non-human creatures. The ability to adapt and create unique voices for each character is a valuable skill in the industry.

Creative Freedom: Voice acting offers a unique creative outlet, allowing actors to bring characters to life using only their voices. It provides an opportunity for imaginative exploration and the freedom to experiment with different vocal choices.

Conclusion

Voice acting is a specialized and rewarding field that requires a unique set of skills. Developing vocal range, flexibility, and control are essential for success in this industry. By mastering techniques such as character analysis, vocal characterization, script interpretation, and mic technique, voice actors can bring characters to life and captivate audiences with their voices alone. While voice acting presents its own challenges, the creative freedom and opportunities for imaginative exploration make it a fulfilling and exciting career path for those passionate about the power of the voice.

PART SEVEN

AUDITIONS AND CASTING

CHAPTER 23 PREPARING FOR AUDITIONS

Auditions are a crucial part of an actor's career. They provide an opportunity to showcase your skills and land the roles you desire. However, auditioning can be a nerve-wracking experience, especially if you are not adequately prepared. In this section, we will explore the essential steps you need to take to prepare for auditions effectively.

Research the Project

Before attending an audition, it is essential to research the project you are auditioning for. This includes understanding the genre, the style of the production, and the character you are auditioning for. Familiarize yourself with the play, film, or TV show and gather as much information as possible. This will help you make informed choices during your audition and demonstrate your understanding of the material.

Read the Script

Once you have gathered information about the project, it is crucial to read the script thoroughly. Take the time to understand the story, the characters, and their relationships. Analyze the scenes that are relevant to your audition and identify the objectives, obstacles, and tactics of your character. This will allow you to make strong choices and bring depth to your performance.

Memorize Your Lines

Memorizing your lines is a fundamental aspect of audition preparation. It is essential to be familiar with the material so that you can focus on your performance rather than struggling to remember your lines. Break down the script into smaller sections and practice each one until you can recite them confidently. Additionally, understanding the context and subtext of your lines will help you deliver a more nuanced performance.

Prepare Your Monologue

In addition to the sides or scenes provided by the casting director, it is beneficial to have a monologue prepared. Choose a monologue that showcases your range and abilities as an actor. Make sure it is appropriate for the project you are auditioning for and aligns with the character you are interested in. Practice your monologue extensively, focusing on your delivery, emotions, and physicality.

Develop Your Character

When preparing for an audition, it is crucial to develop a clear understanding of your character. Dive deep into their background, motivations, and desires. Create a backstory for your character that informs their choices and actions. This will help you bring authenticity and depth to your performance during the audition. Experiment with different choices and interpretations to make your character unique and memorable.

Choose Your Wardrobe

Your wardrobe plays a significant role in auditions, as it helps create a visual impression of your character. Dress appropriately for the role you are auditioning for, considering the time period, setting, and personality of the character. Avoid wearing distracting or overly casual attire that may take away from your performance. Choose clothing that allows you to move comfortably and express yourself physically.

Practice, Practice, Practice

Rehearsing your audition is crucial to build confidence and polish your performance. Practice your scenes, monologues, and any additional material you have prepared. Work on your delivery, timing, and emotional connection to the material. Practice in front of a mirror or record yourself to evaluate your performance objectively. Seek feedback from trusted friends or acting coaches to refine your audition.

Be Prepared for the Unexpected

Auditions can be unpredictable, and you may be asked to perform additional material or make adjustments on the spot. Be prepared for unexpected requests and be flexible in your approach. Stay open to direction and be willing to take risks. The ability to adapt quickly and think on your feet will demonstrate your professionalism and versatility as an actor.

Take Care of Yourself

Preparing for auditions can be mentally and physically demanding. It is crucial to take care of yourself during this process. Get enough rest, eat well, and engage in activities that help you relax and stay focused. Practice self-care techniques such as meditation or deep breathing exercises to manage any anxiety or nerves. Taking care of your well-being will ensure you are in the best possible state to deliver a strong audition.

Arrive Early and Be a Professional

On the day of the audition, make sure to arrive early to allow yourself time to settle and prepare. Dress appropriately and professionally, showing respect for the casting team and the process. Be polite and courteous to everyone you encounter, from the receptionist to the casting director. Remember that auditions are not only about your performance but also about how you present yourself as a professional.

In conclusion, preparing for auditions requires thorough research, script analysis, and extensive practice. By understanding the project, developing your character, and being well-prepared, you can approach auditions with confidence and increase your chances of success. Remember to take care of yourself and maintain a professional attitude throughout the process. With dedication and preparation, you can make the most of every audition opportunity that comes your way.

CHAPTER 24
AUDITION TECHNIQUES

Auditions are a crucial part of an actor's career. It is during auditions that actors have the opportunity to showcase their skills and convince casting directors that they are the right fit for a particular role. However, auditions can also be nerve-wracking and intimidating. In this section, we will explore some audition techniques that can help actors prepare and perform their best during auditions.

Research the Project

Before attending an audition, it is essential to research the project thoroughly. This includes understanding the genre, the style of the production, and the character you are auditioning for. By familiarizing yourself with the project, you can tailor your audition to fit the specific requirements and expectations of the casting team.

Analyze the Script

Once you have a clear understanding of the project, it is crucial to analyze the script. Break down the character's objectives, motivations, and conflicts. Identify the character's arc and how they fit into the overall story. By delving deep into the script, you can bring a more nuanced and informed performance to your audition.

Make Bold Choices

During auditions, casting directors are not only looking for actors who can deliver lines but also for those who can make bold and interesting choices. Don't be afraid to take risks and bring your unique interpretation to the character. Showcasing your creativity and ability to think outside the box can make you stand out from the competition.

Be Prepared

Preparation is key to a successful audition. Memorize your lines thoroughly and practice them until they become second nature. Additionally, be prepared to perform cold readings if required. Familiarize yourself with the sides or scenes provided and practice reading them aloud to ensure you can deliver a convincing performance even without prior preparation.

Use Your Body and Voice

Acting is not just about delivering lines; it is about embodying the character physically and vocally. Use your body language to convey the character's emotions, intentions, and physicality. Pay attention to your posture, gestures, and facial expressions. Similarly, use your voice to bring depth and authenticity to the character. Experiment with different vocal tones, accents, and rhythms to create a compelling performance.

Connect with the Reader

During auditions, you will often be performing in front of a casting director or a reader. It is essential to establish a connection with them and make them feel engaged in your performance. Maintain eye contact, listen actively, and respond to their cues. Treat the reader as your scene partner and create a sense of chemistry and connection between your characters.

Be Flexible and Open to Direction

Casting directors may provide feedback or direction during auditions. It is crucial to be flexible and open to their suggestions. Show that you can take direction and make adjustments to your performance. This demonstrates your ability to collaborate and work well with others, which is highly valued in the industry.

Stay Present and in the Moment

Nerves can often get the best of actors during auditions. To combat this, it is important to stay present and focused in the moment. Ground yourself before entering the audition room by taking deep breaths and centering your energy. Trust in your preparation and let go of any self-doubt. By staying present, you can deliver a more authentic and compelling performance.

Be Professional and Respectful

Professionalism is crucial during auditions. Arrive on time or even a few minutes early to ensure you have ample time to settle in and prepare. Dress appropriately for the role and maintain a positive and respectful attitude towards everyone you encounter, including casting directors, assistants, and fellow actors. Remember that auditions are not just about your talent but also about how you present yourself as a professional.

Learn from Each Audition

Every audition is an opportunity for growth and learning. Regardless of the outcome, take the time to reflect on your performance and identify areas for improvement. Consider seeking feedback from trusted mentors or acting coaches to gain valuable insights. Use each audition experience as a stepping stone towards becoming a better actor.

By incorporating these audition techniques into your preparation and performance, you can increase your chances of making a lasting impression on casting directors. Remember that auditions are not just about getting the role but also about showcasing your skills and building relationships within the industry. Stay dedicated, keep honing your craft, and embrace the journey of auditioning as an integral part of your acting career.

CHAPTER 25
THE CASTING PROCESS

The casting process is a crucial step in the production of any film, television show, or stage production. It involves selecting the right actors to bring the characters to life and play a significant role in the success of the project. Casting directors and producers work together to find the perfect fit for each role, considering various factors such as talent, experience, and chemistry with other cast members. In this section, we will explore the casting process in detail and shed light on the various aspects involved.

The Role of the Casting Director

The casting director plays a pivotal role in the casting process. They are responsible for finding and selecting actors who are suitable for the roles. Casting directors have a deep understanding of the project's requirements and work closely with the director and producers to ensure that the vision for the characters is fulfilled. They often have a vast network of contacts within the industry and may hold auditions or conduct casting calls to discover new talent.

Auditions and Casting Calls

Auditions are a crucial part of the casting process. They provide actors with an opportunity to showcase their skills and suitability for a particular role. Casting directors may hold open auditions or invite specific actors to audition based on their previous work or recommendations. During auditions, actors are typically asked to perform a scene or monologue that demonstrates their range and ability to embody the character.

Casting calls are announcements made to the public, inviting actors to audition for specific roles. These calls may be open to both experienced actors and newcomers, providing an opportunity for fresh talent to be discovered. Actors interested in auditioning for a role typically submit their headshots, resumes, and sometimes a demo reel to the casting director or their team.

Callbacks and Chemistry Readings

After the initial auditions, casting directors may conduct callbacks for selected actors. Callbacks are a chance for the casting team to further assess an actor's suitability for a role. During callbacks, actors may be asked to perform additional scenes or engage in chemistry readings with other actors who have been shortlisted for the project. Chemistry readings are particularly important for roles that require strong on-screen relationships, such as romantic partners or close friends.

Screen Tests and Workshops

For film and television projects, actors who have made it through the audition and callback stages may be asked to participate in screen tests. Screen tests involve filming scenes with the actor to assess their on-camera presence, ability to take direction, and overall suitability for the role. These tests help the director and producers visualize how the actor will appear on screen and how they will bring the character to life.

In some cases, casting directors may also organize workshops or rehearsals with shortlisted actors. These workshops allow the actors to further explore the characters and their dynamics with other cast members. It also provides an opportunity for the director to fine-tune the performances and make any necessary adjustments before filming or production begins.

The Final Decision

Once all the auditions, callbacks, screen tests, and workshops are complete, the casting team, along with the director and producers, make the final decision on casting. They consider various factors, including the actor's talent, suitability for the role, chemistry with other cast members, and overall vision for the project. The final decision is often a collaborative effort, with input from all parties involved.

CHAPTER 26
DEALING WITH REJECTION

Rejection is an inevitable part of the acting industry. No matter how talented or experienced you are, you will face rejection at some point in your career. It can be disheartening and discouraging, but it is important to remember that rejection is not a reflection of your worth as an actor. In this section, we will explore strategies for dealing with rejection and maintaining a positive mindset.

Understanding the Nature of Rejection

Before we delve into coping mechanisms, it is crucial to understand that rejection is a common occurrence in the acting industry. Casting directors have specific visions for their projects, and sometimes you may not fit the desired criteria. It is essential to separate your personal identity from the roles you audition for. Remember that rejection does not define your talent or potential as an actor.

Embracing a Growth Mindset

One of the most effective ways to deal with rejection is to adopt a growth mindset. Instead of viewing rejection as a failure, see it as an opportunity for growth and improvement. Use each rejection as a chance to learn and develop your skills. Analyze your auditions and identify areas where you can enhance your performance. By focusing on self-improvement, you can turn rejection into a catalyst for growth.

Developing Resilience

Resilience is a valuable trait for actors, especially when facing rejection. It is the ability to bounce back from setbacks and maintain a positive attitude. Building resilience takes time and practice, but it is worth the effort. Surround yourself with a supportive network of friends, family, and fellow actors who can provide encouragement and perspective during challenging times. Engage in activities that boost your confidence and help you stay motivated.

Managing Expectations

Setting realistic expectations is crucial when dealing with rejection. Understand that not every audition will result in a role, and that is perfectly normal. Avoid placing too much pressure on yourself and focus on the process rather than the outcome. By managing your expectations, you can approach auditions with a sense of detachment and reduce the impact of rejection on your self-esteem.

Self-care and Emotional Well-being

Rejection can take a toll on your emotional well-being, so it is essential to prioritize self-care. Take time to engage in activities that bring you joy and help you relax. Exercise regularly, eat a balanced diet, and get enough sleep. Surround yourself with positive influences and seek support from friends, family, or a therapist if needed. Taking care of your mental and physical health will help you navigate rejection more effectively.

Reframing Rejection

Instead of viewing rejection as a personal failure, try reframing it as a redirection. Each rejection brings you one step closer to the right opportunity. Embrace the idea that every "no" is leading you towards a "yes." Use rejection as motivation to work harder, refine your skills, and prove yourself. Remember that many successful actors have faced numerous rejections before achieving their breakthrough.

Learning from Rejection

Every audition and rejection is a learning experience. Take the time to reflect on each audition and rejection, and identify areas for improvement. Seek feedback from casting directors or acting coaches to gain valuable insights. Use this feedback constructively to enhance your skills and approach future auditions with a stronger foundation. Learning from rejection can help you grow as an actor and increase your chances of success in the future.

Maintaining a Positive Mindset

Maintaining a positive mindset is crucial when dealing with rejection. Surround yourself with positive influences and engage in activities that uplift your spirits. Practice gratitude and focus on the progress you have made rather than dwelling on rejections. Celebrate small victories and remind yourself of your passion for acting. By cultivating a positive mindset, you can navigate rejection with resilience and determination.

Persistence and Perseverance

Lastly, remember that persistence and perseverance are key to success in the acting industry. Rejection is a natural part of the journey, but it does not define your potential. Stay committed to your craft, continue honing your skills, and keep auditioning. The more auditions you attend, the more opportunities you create for yourself. Stay focused on your goals and believe in your abilities. With persistence and perseverance, you can overcome rejection and achieve your dreams as an actor.

In conclusion, dealing with rejection is an essential skill for actors. By understanding the nature of rejection, embracing a growth mindset, developing resilience, managing expectations, prioritizing self-care, reframing rejection, learning from each experience, maintaining a positive mindset, and persisting in your pursuit, you can navigate rejection with grace and continue to grow as an actor. Remember that rejection is not a reflection of your worth, but rather an opportunity for growth and redirection. Stay focused, stay positive, and keep pursuing your passion for acting.

PART EIGHT

WORKING WITH DIRECTORS AND CO-ACTORS

CHAPTER 27 COLLABORATING WITH DIRECTORS

Collaborating with directors is an essential aspect of an actor's job. Directors play a crucial role in shaping the overall vision and execution of production, and actors must work closely with them to bring their characters to life. This section will explore the importance of collaboration, effective communication, and the dynamics of the actor-director relationship.

The Importance of Collaboration

Collaboration between actors and directors is vital for the success of any production. It is a symbiotic relationship where both parties rely on each other's expertise and creativity. Directors rely on actors to bring their vision to life through their performances, while actors depend on directors for guidance, feedback, and direction.

When actors and directors collaborate effectively, the result is a cohesive and compelling performance. By working together, they can explore different interpretations, experiment with ideas, and find the best way to tell the story. Collaboration allows for a collective effort, where everyone's input is valued and contributes to the overall artistic vision.

Effective Communication

Clear and open communication is the foundation of a successful collaboration between actors and directors. Both parties must be able to express their ideas, concerns, and feedback in a respectful and constructive manner. Effective communication ensures that everyone is on the same page and working towards a common goal.

Actors should be proactive in communicating their thoughts and ideas to the director. They should feel comfortable discussing their character's motivations, intentions, and any questions or concerns they may have. By sharing their insights, actors can contribute to the development of their character and the overall production.

Building Trust and Respect

Trust and respect are essential elements of the actor-director relationship. Actors need to trust that the director has their best interests at heart and will guide them towards delivering their best performance. Directors, on the other hand, need to trust that the actors will fully commit to their roles and bring their characters to life.

Building trust and respect takes time and effort. It requires open and honest communication, active listening, and a willingness to collaborate. Actors should trust that the director's feedback and guidance are meant to enhance their performance, while directors should respect the actors' creative process and individuality.

Understanding the Director's Vision

As an actor, it is crucial to understand and align with the director's vision for the production. Directors have a unique perspective and artistic vision for how they want the story to be told. By understanding their vision, actors can make informed choices that contribute to the overall coherence of the production.

To understand the director's vision, actors should familiarize themselves with the script, the themes, and the director's notes or discussions. They should pay attention to the director's feedback and direction during rehearsals and be open to adapting their performance to align with the overall vision.

Adapting to Different Directing Styles

Every director has their own directing style and approach. Some directors may prefer a more hands-on approach, providing detailed instructions and guidance, while others may take a more collaborative and exploratory approach, allowing actors more freedom to interpret their characters.

As an actor, it is essential to be adaptable and flexible in working with different directing styles. This requires being open to new ideas, taking direction well, and being able to adjust your performance based on the director's feedback. Adapting to different directing styles demonstrates professionalism and a willingness to collaborate.

Navigating Conflicts

Conflicts can arise in any collaborative process, and the actor-director relationship is no exception. Disagreements or differences in opinion may occur, but it is essential to handle conflicts professionally and respectfully.

CHAPTER 28

BUILDING CHEMISTRY WITH CO-ACTORS

Building chemistry with co-actors is an essential aspect of acting that can greatly enhance the overall performance and believability of a scene. When actors have a strong connection and understanding with each other, it creates a sense of authenticity and depth in their performances. This section will explore various techniques and strategies that actors can employ to build chemistry with their co-actors.

Understanding the Importance of Chemistry

The chemistry between co-actors is crucial because it allows them to establish a sense of trust and rapport on stage or on screen. When actors have a genuine connection, it becomes easier for them to react and respond to each other in a natural and organic way. This chemistry can elevate the quality of the performance and make it more compelling for the audience.

Establishing Trust and Communication

One of the first steps in building chemistry with co-actors is establishing trust and open communication. Actors need to create a safe and supportive environment where they can freely express their ideas, concerns, and emotions. This can be achieved through regular rehearsals, discussions, and sharing personal experiences. By getting to know each other on a deeper level, actors can develop a stronger bond and understanding of each other's strengths and weaknesses.

Active Listening and Observation

Actors should practice active listening and observation skills to build chemistry with their co-actors. This involves paying close attention to their partner's cues, body language, and verbal responses. By actively listening, actors can respond authentically and in the moment, creating a more realistic and engaging performance. This level of attentiveness also helps actors adapt and adjust their own performance based on the reactions and energy of their co-actors.

Establishing a Shared Backstory

Creating a shared backstory for the characters can greatly enhance the chemistry between co-actors. By discussing and collaborating on the history and relationship of their characters, actors can develop a deeper understanding of their motivations and dynamics. This shared backstory provides a foundation for the actors to build upon and helps them to establish a more authentic connection on stage or on screen.

Rehearsing Together

Regular rehearsals are essential for building chemistry with co-actors. Through rehearsals, actors have the opportunity to explore different scenes, experiment with different choices, and develop a rhythm and flow in their interactions. Rehearsing together allows actors to become more comfortable with each other's presence and to fine-tune their performances. It also provides an opportunity for actors to give and receive feedback, further strengthening their connection and understanding.

Improvisation and Spontaneity

Incorporating improvisation and spontaneity into rehearsals can be a powerful tool for building chemistry with co-actors. By engaging in improvisational exercises, actors can explore different scenarios and reactions in a spontaneous and unscripted manner. This helps to foster a sense of trust and adaptability between co-actors, as they learn to rely on each other's instincts and responses. Improvisation also encourages actors to be fully present in the moment, creating a more authentic and dynamic performance.

Building Personal Connections

Actors can also build chemistry with their co-actors by developing personal connections outside of rehearsals and performances. Spending time together, engaging in social activities, and getting to know each other on a personal level can strengthen the bond between actors. These personal connections can translate into a more genuine and believable on-stage or on-screen relationship.

Supporting Each Other

Supporting and uplifting each other is crucial for building chemistry with co-actors. Actors should strive to create a positive and encouraging environment where they can celebrate each other's successes and provide constructive feedback when needed. By genuinely supporting and rooting for each other, actors can create a strong sense of camaraderie and teamwork, which ultimately enhances their chemistry on stage or on screen.

Flexibility and Adaptability

Actors should be flexible and adaptable in their approach to building chemistry with co-actors. Each actor has their own unique style and process, and it is important to respect and accommodate these differences. By being open to different ideas and approaches, actors can find common ground and create a harmonious working relationship. Flexibility and adaptability also allow actors to respond to unexpected changes or challenges during performances, further strengthening their chemistry.

Conclusion

Building chemistry with co-actors is a collaborative process that requires trust, communication, and a willingness to connect on a deeper level. By actively listening, observing, and rehearsing together, actors can develop a strong bond and understanding with their co-actors. Creating a shared backstory, incorporating improvisation, and building personal connections also contribute to the chemistry between actors. Ultimately, building chemistry with co-actors enhances the authenticity and believability of performances, creating a more engaging and memorable experience for both the actors and the audience.

CHAPTER 29

ADAPTING TO DIFFERENT DIRECTING STYLES

As an actor, one of the most important skills you can develop is the ability to adapt to different directing styles. Directors have their own unique vision for a production, and it is your job as an actor to understand and execute that vision. Adapting to different directing styles requires flexibility, open-mindedness, and a willingness to collaborate. In this section, we will explore the importance of adapting to different directing styles and provide some tips on how to navigate this aspect of the acting process.

Understanding the Director's Vision

Before you can adapt to a director's style, it is crucial to understand their vision for the production. This involves having open and honest communication with the director, asking questions, and actively listening to their instructions and feedback. Take the time to read the script thoroughly and discuss it with the director to gain a clear understanding of their interpretation and the overall tone they want to achieve.

Researching the Director's Previous Work

Another helpful way to adapt to a director's style is to research their previous work. By watching their past productions or reading reviews, you can gain insight into their artistic preferences, storytelling techniques, and directorial choices. This knowledge can inform your approach and help you align your performance with their vision.

Flexibility in Rehearsals

During rehearsals, directors may experiment with different approaches, techniques, and blocking. It is important to remain flexible and open to trying new things. Be willing to take risks and explore different interpretations of your character. Remember that the rehearsal process is a collaborative effort, and your willingness to adapt and experiment will contribute to the overall success of the production.

Observing and Learning from Co-actors

Working with a diverse group of actors can expose you to different acting styles and approaches. Take the opportunity to observe and learn from your co-actors. Pay attention to how they adapt to the director's style and incorporate their feedback. By observing and learning from others, you can expand your own range as an actor and develop a better understanding of how to adapt to different directing styles.

Adapting to Different Directing Approaches

Directors may have different approaches to working with actors. Some directors prefer a more hands-on approach, providing detailed instructions and guidance throughout the process. Others may take a more collaborative approach, allowing actors more freedom to explore and make choices. It is important to adapt to these different approaches and understand the director's expectations.

If a director is more hands-on, be prepared to take direction and make adjustments based on their feedback. Be open to their suggestions and trust their expertise. Remember that their goal is to bring out the best in your performance and create a cohesive production.

On the other hand, if a director takes a more collaborative approach, be proactive in offering ideas and suggestions. Take ownership of your character and contribute to the creative process. However, always be respectful of the director's ultimate authority and final decisions.

Communication and Collaboration

Effective communication and collaboration are essential when adapting to different directing styles. Be open and honest in your communication with the director, expressing any concerns or questions you may have. Actively listen to their feedback and be receptive to their ideas. Remember that the director's vision is the guiding force behind the production, and your job is to bring that vision to life.

Collaboration extends beyond just the director. It also involves working closely with your co-actors, the production team, and other members of the cast and crew. Building strong relationships and fostering a positive working environment will enhance your ability to adapt to different directing styles and contribute to a successful production.

CHAPTER 30
HANDLING CONFLICTS ON SET

Conflict is an inevitable part of any collaborative process, and the world of acting is no exception. On a film or television set, where multiple individuals with different personalities, opinions, and creative visions come together, conflicts can arise. These conflicts can be between actors, between actors and directors, or even between actors and crew members. It is crucial for actors to develop effective strategies for handling conflicts on set in order to maintain a positive working environment and ensure the success of the project.

Understanding the Nature of Conflict

Before delving into strategies for handling conflicts, it is important to understand the nature of conflict itself. Conflict arises when there is a disagreement or clash of interests between two or more individuals. It can stem from differences in artistic choices, communication breakdowns, ego clashes, or simply misunderstandings. Conflict can be both constructive and destructive, depending on how it is managed. When handled effectively, conflicts can lead to creative solutions, improved relationships, and a stronger final product.

Communication is Key

One of the most important skills an actor can develop to handle conflicts on set is effective communication. Clear and open communication is essential for resolving conflicts and preventing them from escalating. When a conflict arises, it is important to address it promptly and directly, rather than letting it fester and grow. This means expressing your concerns or grievances in a respectful and non-confrontational manner.

Active listening is also crucial in conflict resolution. It involves fully focusing on the other person's perspective, without interrupting or formulating a response in your mind. By actively listening, you demonstrate empathy and understanding, which can help de-escalate the conflict and foster a more collaborative atmosphere.

Seek Common Ground

In the midst of a conflict, it can be easy to focus on differences and become entrenched in your own position. However, seeking common ground can be a powerful tool for resolving conflicts. Look for areas of agreement or shared goals and build upon them. By finding common ground, you can shift the focus from the conflict itself to finding a mutually beneficial solution.

Collaborative Problem-Solving

When conflicts arise, it is important to approach them as opportunities for collaborative problem-solving rather than as battles to be won. Instead of viewing the conflict as a win-lose situation, strive for a win-win outcome where all parties involved feel heard and their needs are met. This requires a willingness to compromise and find creative solutions that address everyone's concerns.

Mediation and Third-Party Intervention

In some cases, conflicts may be too complex or emotionally charged to be resolved through direct communication between the parties involved. In such situations, it can be helpful to involve a neutral third party, such as a mediator or a trusted member of the production team. A mediator can facilitate communication, help identify underlying issues, and guide the parties toward a resolution. Their objective perspective can often bring fresh insights and help break through impasses.

Maintaining Professionalism

In some cases, conflicts may be too complex or emotionally charged to be resolved through direct communication between the parties involved. In such situations, it can be helpful to involve a neutral third party, such as a mediator or a trusted member of the production team. A mediator can facilitate communication, help identify underlying issues, and guide the parties toward a resolution. Their objective perspective can often bring fresh insights and help break through impasses.

Learning from Conflicts

Conflicts, when handled effectively, can be valuable learning experiences. They provide an opportunity for self-reflection and growth, both as an actor and as an individual. After a conflict has been resolved, take the time to reflect on what happened and identify any patterns or triggers that may have contributed to the conflict. This self-awareness can help you navigate future conflicts more effectively and develop stronger interpersonal skills.

Conclusion

Handling conflicts on set is an essential skill for actors. By understanding the nature of conflict, practicing effective communication, seeking common ground, and approaching conflicts as opportunities for collaborative problem-solving, actors can navigate conflicts in a constructive and professional manner. Remember, conflicts are a natural part of the creative process, and by embracing them with a positive mindset, you can contribute to a more harmonious and successful production.

PART NINE

CHALLENGES AND REWARDS OF ACTING

CHAPTER 31

DEALING WITH STAGE FRIGHT

Stage fright, also known as performance anxiety, is a common challenge that many actors face. It is the feeling of nervousness or fear that arises before or during a performance. Stage fright can be overwhelming and can negatively impact an actor's ability to deliver their best performance. However, with the right strategies and techniques, actors can learn to manage and overcome stage fright. In this section, we will explore some effective ways to deal with stage fright and perform with confidence.

Understanding Stage Fright

Before we delve into the strategies to overcome stage fright, it is important to understand its underlying causes. Stage fright is often rooted in the fear of judgment, failure, or embarrassment. It can stem from a lack of self-confidence, fear of making mistakes, or the pressure to meet high expectations. Additionally, the fear of forgetting lines, stumbling on stage, or facing technical difficulties can contribute to stage fright.

Preparation and Rehearsal

One of the most effective ways to combat stage fright is through thorough preparation and rehearsal. The more familiar you are with your lines, blocking, and overall performance, the more confident you will feel on stage. Take the time to study your script, understand your character, and practice your lines until they become second nature. Rehearsing with your fellow actors and receiving feedback can also help build your confidence and reduce anxiety.

Breathing and Relaxation Techniques

Deep breathing and relaxation techniques can be powerful tools in managing stage fright. Before going on stage, take a few moments to focus on your breath. Inhale deeply through your nose, hold for a few seconds, and exhale slowly through your mouth. This can help calm your nerves and reduce tension in your body. Additionally, practicing progressive muscle relaxation, where you tense and release different muscle groups, can help alleviate physical tension and promote relaxation.

Visualization and Positive Affirmations

Visualization is a technique used by many actors to overcome stage fright. Close your eyes and imagine yourself performing confidently and flawlessly on stage. Visualize the audience applauding and cheering for your performance. This mental rehearsal can help build your confidence and reduce anxiety. Alongside visualization, incorporating positive affirmations can be beneficial. Repeat positive statements to yourself, such as "I am a talented actor" or "I am fully prepared for this performance." These affirmations can help shift your mindset from fear to confidence.

Physical Warm-up and Energy Release

Engaging in physical warm-up exercises before a performance can help release nervous energy and reduce tension. Stretching, jogging in place, or doing jumping jacks can help loosen your muscles and increase blood flow. Additionally, engaging in vocal warm-up exercises can help relax your voice and prepare it for the performance. By releasing physical tension and energizing your body, you can alleviate some of the symptoms of stage fright.

Focus on the Character and Story

Shifting your focus from your own anxiety to the character and the story can be helpful in managing stage fright. Remind yourself of the purpose of your performance and the importance of telling the story. By immersing yourself in the character's emotions and motivations, you can redirect your energy towards the performance rather than your fear. Remember that acting is a collaborative art form, and your fellow actors and the audience are there to support and appreciate your work.

Embracing Mistakes and Imperfections

It is important to remember that making mistakes or experiencing imperfections is a natural part of the acting process. No performance is perfect, and even the most experienced actors make errors. Embrace the possibility of mistakes and view them as opportunities for growth and learning. By accepting that imperfections are normal, you can alleviate the pressure to be flawless and focus on delivering an authentic and engaging performance

Seeking Professional Help

If stage fright persists and significantly hinders your ability to perform, it may be beneficial to seek professional help. Acting coaches, therapists, or counselors who specialize in performance anxiety can provide valuable guidance and support. They can help you develop personalized strategies to manage stage fright and build your confidence as an actor.

CHAPTER 32

MAINTAINING EMOTIONAL WELL-BEING

Acting is a profession that requires actors to tap into their emotions and portray a wide range of feelings and experiences. While this can be incredibly rewarding, it can also take a toll on an actor's emotional well-being. It is essential for actors to prioritize their mental and emotional health to ensure they can continue to perform at their best. In this section, we will explore some strategies and techniques that actors can use to maintain their emotional well-being.

Self-Care

Self-care is crucial for actors to maintain their emotional well-being. It involves taking care of oneself physically, mentally, and emotionally. Here are some self-care practices that actors can incorporate into their daily lives:

Physical Health: Engaging in regular exercise, eating a balanced diet, and getting enough sleep are essential for overall well-being. Physical activity can help release endorphins, which are natural mood boosters. Eating nutritious meals and getting sufficient rest can provide actors with the energy they need to perform at their best.

Mental Health: Actors should prioritize their mental health by engaging in activities that promote relaxation and stress reduction. This can include practicing mindfulness or meditation, journaling, or seeking therapy or counseling if needed. Taking breaks from work and engaging in hobbies or activities that bring joy and relaxation can also contribute to mental well-being.

Emotional Health: It is important for actors to acknowledge and process their emotions. This can be done through self-reflection, talking to trusted friends or family members, or seeking professional support if necessary. Engaging in activities that bring joy and fulfillment, such as spending time with loved ones or pursuing hobbies outside of acting, can also contribute to emotional well-being.

CHAPTER 33 BOUNDARIES

Maintaining healthy boundaries is essential for actors to protect their emotional well-being. Acting often requires actors to delve into intense emotions and experiences, which can be emotionally draining. Here are some strategies for setting and maintaining boundaries:

Time Boundaries: Actors should establish a balance between work and personal life. Setting aside designated time for rest, relaxation, and engaging in activities outside of acting can help prevent burnout and maintain emotional well-being.

Emotional Boundaries: It is important for actors to differentiate between their own emotions and those of the characters they portray. While it is necessary to tap into emotions for a convincing performance, actors should be able to detach from those emotions once the scene is over. Developing techniques to separate personal emotions from the characters' emotions can help actors maintain their emotional well-being.

Professional Boundaries: Actors should establish clear boundaries with their colleagues and industry professionals. This can include setting limits on the type of roles they are comfortable with, communicating their needs and concerns, and advocating for themselves in professional settings. Having a strong support system and surrounding oneself with positive and supportive individuals can also contribute to emotional well-being.

Emotional Release Techniques

Actors often experience a range of emotions during their work, and it is important to have healthy outlets for emotional release. Here are some techniques that can help actors process and release emotions:

Journaling: Writing down thoughts and emotions can be a cathartic and therapeutic practice. Actors can use journaling as a tool to reflect on their experiences, process emotions, and gain insights into their own emotional well-being.

Physical Release: Engaging in physical activities such as dancing, yoga, or exercise can help release pent-up emotions and provide a sense of release and relief. Physical movement can also help actors reconnect with their bodies and release tension.

Supportive Networks: Having a strong support system of friends, family, and fellow actors can provide a safe space for actors to express their emotions and seek guidance. Sharing experiences and emotions with others who understand the unique challenges of the acting profession can be incredibly beneficial for emotional well-being.

Seeking Professional Support: Actors may encounter emotional challenges that require professional support. It is important for actors to recognize when they need help and seek assistance from mental health professionals or therapists who specialize in working with performers. These professionals can provide guidance, support, and tools to help actors navigate the emotional demands of their profession.

Conclusion

Maintaining emotional well-being is crucial for actors to thrive in their profession. By practicing self-care, setting boundaries, utilizing emotional release techniques, and seeking professional support when needed, actors can ensure they are taking care of their mental and emotional health. Prioritizing emotional well-being not only benefits actors personally but also enhances their performances and allows them to continue to pursue their passion for acting.

CHAPTER 34

BALANCING PERSONAL AND PROFESSIONAL LIFE

Acting is a demanding profession that requires a significant amount of time, energy, and dedication. It can be challenging to find a balance between your personal life and your career as an actor. However, it is essential to prioritize both aspects of your life to maintain overall well-being and success in your acting journey. In this section, we will explore strategies and tips for balancing your personal and professional life as an actor.

Recognize the Importance of Balance

Balancing personal and professional life is crucial for actors to avoid burnout and maintain a healthy mindset. It is easy to get caught up in the demands of auditions, rehearsals, and performances, but neglecting your personal life can have negative consequences. Remember that your personal life provides the foundation for your happiness and fulfillment, which ultimately enhances your acting abilities.

Set Clear Boundaries

One of the first steps in achieving a balance between personal and professional life is setting clear boundaries. Establishing boundaries helps you prioritize your time and energy effectively. Determine how much time you want to dedicate to your acting career and how much time you want to spend on personal activities, relationships, and self-care. Communicate these boundaries to your agents, directors, and co-actors, so they understand your limitations and respect your personal time.

Prioritize Self-Care

Self-care is essential for maintaining a healthy work-life balance. As an actor, it is crucial to take care of your physical, mental, and emotional well-being. Make time for activities that rejuvenate and relax you, such as exercise, meditation, hobbies, or spending time with loved ones. Prioritizing self-care not only helps you recharge but also enhances your creativity and performance on stage or screen.

Create a Schedule

Creating a schedule is an effective way to manage your time and ensure you allocate enough time for both personal and professional commitments. Plan your days, weeks, and months in advance, including auditions, rehearsals, and performances, as well as personal activities and downtime. Having a schedule allows you to see the big picture and make adjustments when necessary. Be realistic with your time allocation and avoid overcommitting yourself, as it can lead to stress and exhaustion.

Learn to Say No

As an actor, you may feel pressured to say yes to every opportunity that comes your way. However, learning to say no is crucial for maintaining a healthy work-life balance. Evaluate each opportunity carefully and consider how it aligns with your personal and professional goals. Saying no to certain projects or commitments that do not serve your overall well-being allows you to focus on the ones that truly matter and bring you joy.

Delegate and Seek Support

Acting can be a demanding profession, and it is essential to recognize when you need support. Delegate tasks that can be handled by others, such as administrative work or personal errands, to free up your time and energy. Additionally, seek support from friends, family, or fellow actors who understand the challenges you face. Having a support system can provide emotional support, and guidance, and help you navigate the ups and downs of the industry.

Maintain Healthy Relationships

Building and maintaining healthy relationships is vital for a balanced personal and professional life. Surround yourself with supportive and understanding individuals who respect your career and personal commitments. Communicate openly with your loved ones about your schedule, challenges, and needs. Strong relationships provide a sense of stability and support, making it easier to navigate the demands of the acting profession.

CHAPTER 35

FINDING FULFILLMENT IN ACTING

Acting is a unique and rewarding profession that allows individuals to express themselves creatively and connect with audiences on a deep emotional level. While the journey of becoming an actor can be challenging, the fulfillment that comes from pursuing this passion is unparalleled. In this section, we will explore the various aspects of finding fulfillment in acting and how actors can navigate the ups and downs of their careers.

The Joy of Self-Expression

One of the most fulfilling aspects of acting is the opportunity it provides for self-expression. Through embodying different characters and exploring their emotions, actors can tap into their own inner world and share it with others. This process allows actors to connect with their own vulnerabilities, strengths, and experiences, ultimately leading to personal growth and self-discovery.

One of the most fulfilling aspects of acting is the opportunity it provides for self-expression. Through embodying different characters and exploring their emotions, actors can tap into their own inner world and share it with others. This process allows actors to connect with their own vulnerabilities, strengths, and experiences, ultimately leading to personal growth and self-discovery.

Acting also offers a platform to address important social issues and provoke thought and discussion. By portraying diverse characters and telling compelling stories, actors have the power to inspire change and make a positive impact on society. This ability to use their craft as a means of communication and advocacy can bring immense fulfillment and purpose to an actor's life.

Creating Meaningful Connections

Acting is a collaborative art form that requires actors to work closely with directors, co-actors, and the entire production team. Through this collaboration, actors have the opportunity to form deep and meaningful connections with their fellow artists. The bonds formed during rehearsals and performances can be incredibly fulfilling, as actors support and inspire each other to create something truly special.

Furthermore, acting allows actors to connect with audiences on a profound level. The ability to evoke emotions and provoke empathy in viewers can create a sense of fulfillment and purpose. Knowing that their performances have touched the hearts of others and made a lasting impact can be incredibly rewarding for actors.

Personal Growth and Development

Acting is a continuous journey of growth and development. As actors take on different roles and explore various techniques, they are constantly challenging themselves and expanding their skills. This process of self-improvement can lead to a deep sense of fulfillment and accomplishment.

Through the exploration of different characters, actors gain a deeper understanding of human nature and the complexities of the human experience. This heightened awareness and empathy can not only enhance their performances but also enrich their personal lives. The ability to see the world through different perspectives and understand the intricacies of human behavior can be incredibly fulfilling and transformative.

Overcoming Challenges

While acting can be immensely fulfilling, it is not without its challenges. Actors often face rejection, competition, and the pressure to constantly prove themselves. However, it is through these challenges that actors can find even greater fulfillment.

By embracing the ups and downs of their career, actors develop resilience and determination. Each audition, performance, and setback becomes an opportunity for growth and learning. Overcoming obstacles and persevering in the face of adversity can bring a profound sense of fulfillment and pride.

Finding Balance

Finding fulfillment in acting also involves finding a balance between personal and professional life. The demands of the profession can be intense, with long hours, irregular schedules, and the need to constantly be "on." However, it is crucial for actors to prioritize self-care and maintain a healthy work-life balance.

Taking time for rest, relaxation, and pursuing other interests outside of acting can prevent burnout and contribute to overall fulfillment. Engaging in activities that bring joy and fulfillment outside of the acting world can provide a sense of grounding and perspective.

Conclusion

Finding fulfillment in acting is a deeply personal and individual journey. It involves embracing the joy of self-expression, creating meaningful connections, experiencing personal growth, overcoming challenges, and finding balance. By navigating these aspects of the acting profession, actors can discover a sense of purpose, fulfillment, and satisfaction in their craft.

PART TEN

CONTINUING EDUCATION AND GROWTH

CHAPTER 36

ACTING CLASSES AND WORKSHOPS

Acting is a craft that requires continuous learning and growth. Even the most experienced actors understand the importance of honing their skills and staying updated with the latest techniques and trends in the industry. One of the most effective ways to achieve this is by enrolling in acting classes and workshops.

The Benefits of Acting Classes and Workshops

Acting classes and workshops offer numerous benefits to actors at all stages of their careers. Here are some of the key advantages:

Skill Development: Acting classes provide a structured environment for actors to develop and refine their skills. Whether it's improving their emotional range, physicality, voice projection, or character development, these classes offer targeted exercises and techniques to enhance specific aspects of acting.

Experimentation and Exploration: Classes and workshops provide a safe space for actors to experiment with different acting styles and techniques. They can explore various approaches to character development, improvisation, and scene work, allowing them to expand their range and discover new ways of expressing themselves.

Feedback and Critique: One of the most valuable aspects of acting classes is the opportunity to receive feedback and critique from experienced instructors and fellow actors. Constructive criticism helps actors identify their strengths and weaknesses, enabling them to grow and improve their performances.

Networking and Collaboration: Acting classes and workshops bring together actors from diverse backgrounds and experiences. This creates a valuable networking opportunity, allowing actors to connect with like-minded individuals, potential collaborators, and even industry professionals. Collaborating with other actors in-class exercises and scene work also helps develop the essential skill of working with co-actors.

Confidence Building: Acting classes and workshops provide a safe and nurturing space for actors to step out of their comfort zones and take risks. Through various exercises and scene work, actors can explore different characters, emotions, and situations. This process helps build confidence and self-assurance, enabling actors to fully embody their roles and deliver authentic performances. The supportive environment of a class or workshop allows actors to make mistakes, learn from them, and grow as performers.

Choosing the Right Acting Classes and Workshops

When selecting acting classes and workshops, it is important to consider your goals, interests, and skill level. Here are some factors to consider:

Curriculum and Focus: Different acting classes and workshops may have varying curriculums and areas of focus. Some may emphasize scene work, while others may focus on specific techniques or genres. Consider what aspects of acting you want to improve or explore and choose classes that align with your interests and goals.

Instructor Experience and Reputation: Research the instructors leading the classes or workshops. Look for instructors with extensive experience in the industry and a strong reputation for their teaching abilities. Reading reviews or seeking recommendations from other actors can help you gauge the quality of instruction.

Class Size and Structure: Consider the class size and structure that suits your learning style. Some actors thrive in smaller, more intimate settings, while others prefer larger groups. Additionally, consider the duration and frequency of the classes or workshops. Determine whether you prefer a short-term intensive workshop or a longer-term class that meets regularly.

Cost and Accessibility: Take into account the cost of the classes or workshops and ensure they fit within your budget. Consider the location and accessibility of the classes, as well as any additional expenses such as travel or accommodation.

Conclusion

Acting classes and workshops are invaluable resources for actors at all stages of their careers. They provide a supportive and structured environment for skill development, feedback, and networking. By enrolling in acting classes and workshops, actors can continue to grow, expand their skill set, and stay inspired in their pursuit of the craft. So, whether you are a beginner or an experienced actor, consider investing in your craft by enrolling in acting classes and workshops.

CHAPTER 37
EXPANDING YOUR SKILL SET

As an actor, it is essential to continuously expand your skill set to stay competitive in the industry and to grow as an artist. While mastering a specific acting method is valuable, it is equally important to explore and incorporate various techniques into your repertoire. This section will discuss the importance of expanding your skill set as an actor and provide some practical ways to do so.

The Benefits of Expanding Your Skill Set

Expanding your skill set as an actor offers several benefits. Firstly, it allows you to approach different roles and characters with versatility and adaptability. Each character is unique, and having a diverse range of skills will enable you to bring authenticity and depth to your performances.

Secondly, expanding your skill set opens up more opportunities for you as an actor. Casting directors and directors are often looking for actors who can bring something fresh and unique to their projects. By having a wide range of skills, you increase your chances of being considered for a variety of roles in different mediums, such as stage, film, television, and voice acting.

Furthermore, expanding your skill set helps you to continue growing as an artist. It keeps your passion for acting alive and challenges you to explore new techniques and approaches. By constantly learning and evolving, you can avoid falling into a creative rut and continue to push the boundaries of your craft.

Practical Ways to Expand Your Skill Set

Take Acting Classes and Workshops: One of the most effective ways to expand your skill set is by enrolling in acting classes and workshops. Look for reputable institutions or acting schools that offer a wide range of courses. Consider exploring different acting methods, such as the Stanislavski System, Meisner Technique, Method Acting, and Brechtian Approach. Each method has its own unique principles and exercises that can enhance your acting abilities.

Study Different Acting Styles: Familiarize yourself with various acting styles from different cultures and time periods. This can include classical acting, contemporary acting, physical theater, improvisation, and more. By studying different styles, you can broaden your understanding of acting techniques and incorporate elements from different traditions into your performances.

Learn Other Performance Skills: Expand your skill set by learning other performance skills that complement acting. This can include singing, dancing, stage combat, acrobatics, or even playing a musical instrument. These additional skills can make you a more well-rounded performer and open up opportunities in musical theater, physical theater, or other performance-based mediums.

Explore Different Genres and Characters: Challenge yourself by exploring different genres and characters that are outside your comfort zone. If you primarily work in drama, try your hand at comedy or vice versa. Experiment with playing characters of different ages, backgrounds, and personalities. This will not only expand your skill set but also help you discover new aspects of your own abillties as an actor.

Collaborate with Other Artists: Seek opportunities to collaborate with other artists from different disciplines. This can include working with directors, playwrights, choreographers, and visual artists. Collaborative projects can expose you to new perspectives and approaches to storytelling, enriching your own artistic process.

Attend Industry Events and Festivals: Participate in industry events, such as film festivals, theater festivals, and acting conferences. These events provide opportunities to network with other actors, directors, and industry professionals. Engaging in conversations and attending workshops or panel discussions can expose you to new ideas and techniques.

Read Plays and Scripts: Expand your knowledge of different playwrights, scripts, and dramatic literature. Reading plays from various genres and time periods can expose you to different storytelling techniques and character dynamics. It can also inspire you to explore new approaches to interpreting and portraying characters.

Experiment with Different Mediums: If you primarily work in one medium, such as stage acting, consider exploring other mediums like film, television, or voice acting. Each medium has its own unique requirements and techniques. By gaining experience in different mediums, you can expand your skill set and increase your versatility as an actor.

Remember, expanding your skill set as an actor is a lifelong journey. Embrace the opportunity to learn and grow, and never stop challenging yourself. By continuously expanding your skill set, you can become a well-rounded and versatile actor, ready to take on any role that comes your way.

CHAPTER 37
NETWORKING AND BUILDING CONNECTIONS

Networking and building connections are essential aspects of an actor's career. In the entertainment industry, who you know can often be just as important as what you know. Building a strong network of contacts can open doors to new opportunities, help you find representation, and lead to collaborations with other talented individuals. In this section, we will explore the importance of networking, strategies for building connections, and how to make the most of these relationships.

The Power of Networking

Networking is the process of establishing and nurturing relationships with individuals who can potentially assist you in your acting career. It involves connecting with industry professionals, fellow actors, casting directors, agents, producers, and anyone else who can provide valuable insights or opportunities. Networking is not about using people for personal gain but rather about building genuine connections based on mutual respect and shared interests.

One of the primary benefits of networking is the access it provides to insider information. By connecting with people who are already established in the industry, you can gain valuable insights into upcoming auditions, casting calls, and industry trends. Additionally, networking allows you to learn from the experiences of others, providing you with valuable advice and guidance as you navigate your own acting journey.

Strategies for Building Connections

Building connections in the acting industry requires a proactive approach. Here are some strategies to help you effectively network and build meaningful relationships:

Attend Industry Events: Make an effort to attend industry events such as film festivals, acting workshops, and networking mixers. These events provide opportunities to meet industry professionals and fellow actors in a more relaxed and social setting.

Join Acting Organizations: Consider joining acting organizations or unions that provide networking opportunities and resources for actors. These organizations often host events, workshops, and seminars that can help you connect with industry professionals.

Utilize Social Media: Social media platforms like LinkedIn, Instagram, Facebook, and Twitter can be powerful tools for networking. Follow industry professionals, engage with their content, and participate in online discussions. Additionally, consider creating a professional website or online portfolio to showcase your work and make it easier for others to find and connect with you.

Collaborate with Others: Seek out opportunities to collaborate with other actors, directors, and filmmakers. By working on projects together, you can build relationships and expand your network. Attend local theater productions, independent film screenings, and acting classes to meet like-minded individuals who share your passion for the craft.

Volunteer and Assist: Offer your assistance on film sets, theater productions, or other industry-related events. Volunteering not only allows you to gain valuable experience but also provides an opportunity to connect with industry professionals and demonstrate your dedication and work ethic.

Maintain Professionalism: When networking, it is crucial to maintain a professional demeanor. Be respectful, punctual, and reliable. Treat every interaction as an opportunity to make a positive impression and build a lasting connection.

Making the Most of Your Connections

Building connections is only the first step; it is equally important to nurture and maintain these relationships. Here are some tips for making the most of your connections:

Follow-Up: After meeting someone at an event or connecting online, follow up with a personalized message expressing your gratitude for the interaction. This simple gesture can help solidify the connection and keep the lines of communication open.

Stay in Touch: Regularly reach out to your connections to check in, share updates on your career, and offer support. Remember, networking is a two-way street, so be willing to provide assistance or advice when needed.

Be Genuine: Authenticity is key when building connections. Be yourself and show a genuine interest in others. People are more likely to remember and support those who are sincere and authentic.

Attend Industry Functions: Stay active in the industry by attending industry functions, premieres, and screenings. These events provide opportunities to reconnect with your network and meet new industry professionals.

Pay It Forward: As you progress in your career, remember to pay it forward by helping aspiring actors and industry newcomers. Share your knowledge and experiences, offer mentorship, and provide support to those who are just starting their journey.

Networking and building connections are ongoing processes throughout an actor's career. By actively engaging in networking activities, nurturing relationships, and making the most of your connections, you can create a strong support system that will help propel your acting career forward. Remember, the entertainment industry is built on relationships, and the connections you make can play a significant role in your success.

CHAPTER 38
STAYING INSPIRED AND MOTIVATED

Acting is a demanding and challenging profession that requires constant inspiration and motivation. As an actor, it is essential to stay inspired and motivated to continue growing and evolving in your craft. In this section, we will explore some strategies and techniques to help you stay inspired and motivated throughout your acting journey.

Find Your Passion: One of the most effective ways to stay inspired and motivated as an actor is to connect with your passion for the craft. Take some time to reflect on why you chose acting as a career and what it means to you. Rediscover the joy and excitement that acting brings to your life. When you are passionate about what you do, it becomes easier to stay motivated and overcome any challenges that come your way.

Set Goals: Setting goals is crucial for staying motivated and focused on your acting career. Start by defining both short-term and long-term goals. Short-term goals can be as simple as learning a new acting technique or attending a specific workshop. Long-term goals may include landing a lead role in a play or film, or even starting your own production company. Having clear goals gives you something to work towards and keeps you motivated to push yourself further.

Surround Yourself with Inspiration: Surrounding yourself with inspiration can greatly impact your motivation as an actor. Seek out opportunities to watch live performances, whether it's attending plays, musicals, or improv shows. Watching other actors in action can ignite your creativity and remind you of the power of storytelling. Additionally, reading books, watching films, and exploring different art forms can also provide inspiration and fuel your passion for acting.

Stay Educated: Continuing your education and learning new skills is essential for staying inspired and motivated as an actor. Take acting classes and workshops regularly to expand your knowledge and improve your craft. Explore different acting techniques and styles to keep your approach fresh and exciting. Learning from experienced teachers and industry professionals can provide valuable insights and reignite your enthusiasm for acting.

Embrace Challenges: Challenges are inevitable in any artistic pursuit, including acting. Instead of being discouraged by them, embrace challenges as opportunities for growth and learning. Push yourself out of your comfort zone and take on roles or projects that challenge you as an actor. Embracing challenges not only helps you develop new skills but also keeps your passion for acting alive by constantly pushing your boundaries.

Stay Connected with the Acting Community: Building connections and staying connected with the acting community is vital for staying inspired and motivated. Attend industry events, join acting organizations, and participate in networking opportunities. Surrounding yourself with like-minded individuals who share your passion for acting can provide support, encouragement, and valuable insights. Collaborating with other actors and creatives can also spark new ideas and keep your motivation levels high.

Take Care of Yourself: Acting can be physically and emotionally demanding, so it's crucial to prioritize self-care. Take care of your physical health by exercising regularly, eating nutritious meals, and getting enough rest. Engage in activities that help you relax and recharge, such as meditation, yoga, or hobbies outside of acting. Taking care of your mental and emotional well-being is equally important. Seek support from friends, family, or a therapist when needed, and practice self-reflection to maintain a healthy mindset.

Celebrate Your Achievements: Acknowledge and celebrate your achievements along the way. Acting is a challenging profession, and it's important to recognize your progress and successes, no matter how small they may seem. Celebrating your achievements not only boosts your confidence but also serves as a reminder of why you chose this path. It can reignite your motivation and inspire you to keep striving for excellence.

Stay Positive and Grateful: Maintaining a positive mindset and practicing gratitude can significantly impact your motivation as an actor. Focus on the positive aspects of your acting journey and be grateful for the opportunities and experiences that come your way. Surround yourself with positive influences and avoid negativity that can drain your motivation. Cultivating a positive and grateful attitude will help you stay inspired and motivated even during challenging times.

Keep Evolving: Finally, remember that growth and evolution are essential in any artistic pursuit. Continuously challenge yourself to learn and grow as an actor. Experiment with different genres, styles, and mediums to expand your skill set. Embrace feedback and constructive criticism as opportunities for improvement. By constantly evolving and pushing your boundaries, you will stay inspired and motivated to reach new heights in your acting career.

In conclusion, staying inspired and motivated as an actor is crucial for your growth and success in the industry. Find your passion, set goals, surround yourself with inspiration, stay educated, embrace challenges, stay connected with the acting community, take care of yourself, celebrate your achievements, stay positive and grateful, and keep evolving. By implementing these strategies, you will maintain a strong sense of inspiration and motivation throughout your acting journey.

NOTES

NOTES

NOTES

NOTES

NOTES

thank you

Dear Reader,

I want to express my deepest gratitude to each one of you for embarking on this journey through the world of acting with my book. Your support and enthusiasm have meant the world to me.

Acting is a craft that thrives on passion and dedication, and I hope my words have ignited that spark within you. Whether you're a seasoned actor or just beginning to explore this incredible art form, your commitment to honing your skills is truly commendable.

Thank you for allowing me to be a part of your artistic growth. May the pages of this book continue to inspire and guide you as you tread the boards of life's grandest stage.

With heartfelt appreciation,

Kedar

THIS
IS
THE
FIRST
BOOK
I
WROTE
HOPE
YOU
LIKED IT